IWAIN

A STUDY IN THE ORIGINS OF ARTHURIAN ROMANCE.

ARTHUR C. L. BROWN

HASKELL HOUSE PUBLISHERS LTD.
Publishers of Scarce Scholarly Books
NEW YORK. N. Y. 10012
1968

First Published 1903

HASKELL HOUSE PUBLISHERS Ltd.
Publishers of Scarce Scholarly Books
280 LAFAYETTE STREET
NEW YORK, N. Y. 10012

Library of Congress Catalog Card Number: 68-8365

Haskell House Catalogue Item # 515

Printed in the United States of America

CONTENTS.

I.

IWAIN

A STUDY IN THE ORIGINS OF ARTHURIAN ROMANCE.
ARTHUR C. L. BROWN

II.

ARTHUR AND GORLAGON
G. L. Kittredge

PREFATORY NOTE TO *IWAIN*.

THIS study, in a form somewhat more extended, was presented in May, 1900, to the Faculty of Arts and Sciences of Harvard University in fulfillment of a requirement made of candidates for the degree of Doctor of Philosophy. The manuscript was revised and sent to the composing room in this same year, and has been in type for a long time. Hence it has been impossible to insert references to a number of recent books and articles.

The object of the dissertation is to investigate the vexed question of the sources of Chrétien's *Ivain*. No attempt has been made to pursue the study of Iwain through the later romances,[1] though that would without doubt lead to interesting results. Nor has any discussion been attempted of the exact relations of the versions of the story in the different languages of Western Europe, or of the still-disputed question of the connection between the Welsh *Owein and Lunet* and the French poem. It did not appear that those subjects could be treated with absolute thoroughness until the real nature of the story of the *Ivain* had been determined,—that is to say, until the question of the sources of the *Ivain* had been settled, at least so far as the nature of the evidence admitted. It was felt that this could

---

[1] To the section on the Giant Herdsman (pp. 70–74) ought to be added a note referring to the *Livre d'Artus*, MS. P (summarized by Freymond, *Zt. f. franz. Sprache*, XVII, 1–128, 1895), where is an account of a combat at a fountain that exhibits almost verbal borrowings from the *Ivain*, but changes the story in certain striking particulars. The Huge Herdsman is expressly said to be Merlin in disguise, who has assumed this shape in order to lead Calogrenant to the fountain. This passage in the *Livre d'Artus* proves that the wood-monster in Chrétien's *Ivain* was easily understood as somebody in disguise.

only be done by a study of all accessible Celtic other-world stories, whether Irish or Welsh, and an investigation of the primitive character and the development of that particular type of " fairy mistress " story which it might appear that the *Ivain* most resembled.   This is the object of the present discussion, and all other questions have been subordinated.

It is believed that the results have justified the undertaking.   Not only does the supposed connection of the *Ivain* with *The Matron of Ephesus* appear to be disproved, but the theory of a Celtic origin for the *Ivain* story has, it is thought, been established beyond a reasonable doubt.   It is hoped that the following pages may also be of service in throwing some new light on the nature of Celtic fairy tales and in pointing out new parallels between Irish and Welsh literature.

I wish to express my hearty thanks to Professor Schofield, who suggested the subject of this investigation and has continually aided me with friendly criticism and advice ; and to Professor Kittredge and Professor Sheldon, who have given me invaluable direction and have permitted me to draw upon their time and scholarship in many ways.   All three, with Professor Robinson, have had the great kindness to read the entire paper in proof.

I am also indebted for various services to Professor Arthur R. Marsh, Professor G. W. Benedict of Brown University, Professor W. D. Howe of the University of Indianapolis, Dr. Alma Blount, formerly of Radcliffe College, Professor R. H. Fletcher of Washington University, and Professor E. F. Langley of Dartmouth College.

A. C. L. B.

THE UNIVERSITY OF WISCONSIN,
        March 15, 1903.

IWAIN.

CHAPTER I.

DEFINITE study of the sources of Chrétien's *Ivain* is not very old. The earliest discussion of the subject that requires mention here was that of Rauch[1] in 1869. Rauch argued that the Welsh *Owein and Lunet* is not the source of Chrétien's *Ivain*, as La Villemarqué and other earlier writers had supposed, but that both tales go back to a common original. This common original must, he thought, have been "eine zum Zweck des Erzählens zusammengestellte Sammlung mehrerer in verschiedenen Zeiten entstandener Erzählungen" (p. 11), which had perhaps no other connection than that they all dealt with a knight called Iwain. One of these stories, that of the Fountain, repeats itself in true *märchen* style "nach der Weise des Volksmärchens unermüdlich mit derselben Ausführlichkeit und denselben refrainartig wiederkehrenden Ausdrücken," and contains in the Welsh version some very primitive features. For example, "es zeigt uns die Königin mit ihren Frauen am Fenster des Saales Nadelarbeit verrichtend, während der König in demselben Raume schlummert." Rauch regarded it as certain, therefore, that this part of the story at least is a Celtic tale much older than the period of Chrétien de Troies.

In 1879 Blume brought into prominence a comparison between Laudine and the theme of the Easily Consoled Widow. Blume

---

[1] *Die wälische, französische und deutsche Bearbeitung der Iweinsage*, Berlin, 1869. Holland, *Crestien von Troies*, Tübingen, 1854, should perhaps be mentioned also; see especially p. 171.

I

quoted[1] from Gervinus, who had expressed himself[2] as shocked by the sudden change of feeling experienced by Laudine, and added : " Aber war Gervinus denn die Geschichte von der treulosen Witwe[3] unbekannt, die in den Literaturen aller Zeiten und Völker begegnet und also doch wohl in der Psychologie des Weibes ihre Erklärung finden muss ? Hat er vergessen, wie die Prinzessin Anna bei Shakespeare sich von Richard von Gloster kirren lässt ? "

In 1883 Goossens[4] published a dissertation in which he undertook to deal with the whole question concerning Iwain. He thinks the kernel of the story was a folk-tale localized in Brittany, about a wonderful fountain that revenged itself on its profaner. In the course of time, he thinks, the punishment became personified in the knight whom Iwain slew. He thinks that Chrétien heard the story from a Breton bard, and that the Welsh version is founded on some French form of the Breton tale. The story, as told by the bards, was probably well settled in its main features, but Chrétien doubtless altered it somewhat. He put in many reflective passages, enriched the dialogue, and introduced the courtly manners of his time. On the whole, however, the *Ivain* is a string of adventures somewhat disconnected and not entirely understood by the author.

In 1884 appeared the first[5] of the excellent editions of the works of Chrétien prepared by Professor Wendelin Foerster. In his introduction this scholar adopted the unfortunate idea that the kernel of the *Ivain* is the theme of the Easily Consoled Widow, an idea that he has ever since defended with much vigor. He says : " Sehen wir schärfer zu, so finden wir, dass, abgesehen von der Oertlichkeit (Broceliande u. s. f.) und den Namen der handelnden Personen, keine Spur von keltischem Stoff zu finden ist, und — vielleicht ist dies ein nicht zu unterschätzendes Moment — es fehlt auch thatsächlich jede

---

[1] *Ueber den Iwein des Hartmann von Aue, ein Vortrag*, p. 19.

[2] *Geschichte der deutschen Dichtung*, 4th ed., 1853, I, 371.

[3] The comparison of Laudine to the Widow of Ephesus was first suggested by Simrock, *Altdeutsches Lesebuch in neudeutscher Sprache*, Stuttgart, 1854, p. 230 (quoted by Holland, *Crestien von Troies*, 1854, p. 158).

[4] Heinrich Goossens, *Ueber Sage, Quelle und Komposition des Chevalier au Lyon des Crestien de Troyes*, Paderborn, 1883.

[5] *Cligés*, Christian von Troyes, *Sämtliche Werke*, I.

Erwähnung und Anspielung auf eine vom Dichter benutzte Quelle. Der Kern des Löwenritters ist vielmehr ein alter Bekannter, ᵣr aus weiter Ferne auf vielen Umwegen nach Frankreich gekon. ᵣn war, nemlich die Sage von der leicht getrösteten Wittwe, die in der Variante der '*Matrone von Ephesus*' am bekanntesten ist. Um diesen Kern ist alles andere gewickelt. Aber welch eine wahrhaft geniale Kunst, diesen abgedroschenen, plumpen Stoff zu behandeln ! ... Um diesen Kern gruppirt nun Christian den König Artus und seinen Hof, er führt uns an die Zauberquelle im Wald Broceliande, er führt uns Riesen im Kampfe vor, lässt uns in die (schon damals existirende) Sklaverei der Fabriken (hier eine Seidenweberei) einen flüchtigen Blick werfen — aber all dies ist nichts als Beiwerk, ange- than, um sich gewogene Leser zu verschaffen, die alle den modernsten aller Stoffe, die grösste '*actualité*,' nemlich die Artussage, heissgierig verlangten. Allein um dem Roman die richtige Länge zu geben, greift der Dichter zu einem von ihm bereits früher (*Erec*) behandelten Thema, dem 'Verliegen' des Ritters, das er diesmal (mit Erec ver- glichen) auf den Kopf stellt und so lässt er den glücklichen Bräutigam, eben dass er sich nicht 'verliege,' gleich nach der Hochzeit in die Welt auf Abenteuer ziehen " (pp. xvi–xvii). Foerster adds that *Cligés* is made out of the well-known story of the " betrogener Ehemann," just as *Ivain* is made out of the " Matrone von Ephesus."

In his edition of *Ivain* in 1887 Foerster reiterated this opinion about the source of the story, adding the following remarks [1]: "Über die Eigenart der echten keltischen Sagenstoffe kann man sich wohl ein Urteil aus der Vergleichung der vorhandenen, gesicherten Proben, wie Melion und den damit eng verwandten Bisclavret, Yonec, Corn, Ignaure, Tydorel,[2] machen. Allen ist das Übernatürliche gemeinsam : Wehrwolf, Zaubertrank, Fee u. dgl. oder grausiger Mord und andere fremdartige Dinge. Jedermann denkt sofort an die Zauberquelle, den Zauberring Lunetens (vgl. aber Gyges) und auch ich habe nichts dagegen, dieses Beiwerk als keltisch gelten zu lassen ebenso wie den

---

[1] *Der Löwenritter*, Christian von Troyes, *Sämtliche erhaltene Werke*, II, xxii– xxiv.

[2] In a footnote Foerster remarks : " Selbst Tristan kann ich nicht für keltisch halten."

Riesen, den Yvain besiegt. Zuletzt käme Artus und sein Hof, deren keltischer Ursprung nicht geläugnet werden kann; man nehme aber statt dessen fränkische, griechische oder römische Namen und Lokalitäten, und die ganze Geschichte bleibt dieselbe. Es ist also rein äussere Zuthat. — Damit ist aber auch alles keltische erschöpft, und man muss zugeben, dass diese Elemente fehlen können, ohne dass der Yvain darunter litte. Die Quelle von Broceliande gibt dem Dichter bloss die Gelegenheit, seinen Helden mit der Heldin in Verbindung zu bringen, wie der Galgen und das Grab; er konnte ebensogut ein anderes Mittel wählen. Der Riese ist nur eine Nummer mehr in der Reihe der von Yvain bestandenen Abenteuer und hat mit der Erzählung überhaupt gar nichts weiter gemein. Allein der Kern selbst, dass nämlich die Heldin den *Mörder* ihres geliebten Gatten heiratet, scheint keltisch sein zu können: allein es ist, wie ich oben bemerkt, ein internationaler Sagenstoff, der in Frankreich durch die Fabeldichtung längst bekannt war, bevor die matiere de Bretagne anfing, dort Aufnahme zu finden. Doch selbst zugegeben, dass Christian diesen Stoff durch Vermittlung der bretonischen Legende erhalten haben sollte, hätte er ihn doch selbständig verarbeitet, und sein Verdienst ist daher in beiden Fällen dasselbe. Denn die Art, wie Christian diesen Kern zur Schürzung und Lösung des Knotens verwendet, ist eine solche, dass sie, inhaltlich betrachtet, keltisch *nicht sein kann*. Der Held nimmt, um durch Verliegen seinen Ritterwert nicht einzubüssen, Urlaub von der eben gewonnenen Gattin und zieht auf Abenteuer aus. Er lässt die ihm bewilligte Frist verstreichen und, von der Gattin verstossen, wird er wahnsinnig.[1] Durch eine Zaubersalbe Morgan's der Fee (er konnte

---

[1] Foerster here adds a note which shows his characteristic method of reasoning about this subject: "Dieses Motiv kehrt auch sonst in Artusromanen wieder. Ist es keltisch oder hat Christian es zuerst angewandt und so in die Artuslitteratur eingeführt? Fragen, die sich nicht entscheiden lassen, die aber unsere Ansicht nicht beeinträchtigen." Foerster is evidently entirely at a loss to explain the "madness motive," and yet it is evident that any theory, to hold its ground, *must* explain such a curious feature of the story as this. He continues: "Die keltische Legende (wenn es wirklich eine solche gegeben hat, die zu den Franzosen gekommen) kann im besten Fall nur die einzelnen Mosaiksteinchen geliefert haben, daraus dann die französischen Künstler die feinen bunten Gemälde

natürlich auch anders genesen oder gar nicht wahnsinnig werden : blosser Zierrat) genesen, erwirbt er sich unter dem fremden Namen des Löwenritters hohen Ruhm und wird endlich, ohne eigentliche Sühne, äusserlich durch einen Kunstgriff der Zofe, mit seiner Herrin wieder ausgesöhnt. Diese beiden treibenden Ideen nun: ' Verliegen und Ritterehre' sind *rein französisch*,[1] und können daher ebenso wenig aus der Bretagne (sei es der grossen und der kleinen) stammen, wie der vom Helden befreite und ihn begleitende Löwe, der zwar in Nordafrica (Androclus !) vorkommt, aber nicht bei den Kelten."

These views of Foerster's were speedily objected to by Gaston Paris.[2] Paris said : "Je crois qu'il va trop loin dans la réaction légitime qu'a provoquée le celticisme à outrance ; mais c'est là une question qui demande un examen long et spécial. Je me borne ici à remarquer que je ne comprends pas comme M. F. le sujet primitif du récit que Chrétien a mis en vers. Il y voit une variante du conte de la *Matrone d'Ephèse ;* j'y vois bien plutôt une forme altérée du thème que nous retrouvons dans *Guingamor*, dans *Oger le danois*, dans *Tanhäuser*, etc. : le héros quitte une fée, dont il est devenu

---

zusammenstellten " (p. xxiii). So far as this means that Chrétien dressed up his Celtic material in the costume of the age of chivalry, it is certainly justified, but the figure of a mosaic made up of stones gathered here and there is an unwarranted one to use till it has first been proved that Chrétien could not have found the greater part at least of the separate incidents of the *Ivain* already in combination. *A priori*, the probabilities are against any patchwork theory.

[1] Foerster's main argument against the Celtic theory is really that the Arthurian romances in the form in which they have come down to us are full of the ideas of the age of chivalry, and therefore can have no foundation in rude antiquity. I have already called attention to the weakness of this argument, in an article (*The Round Table before Wace*) in *Harvard Studies and Notes*, VII, 193–194, note : " It is not true, as has been sometimes carelessly maintained, that the chivalrous setting in which Arthurian stories have come down to us disproves their foundation in rude antiquity. A primitive story may be beautified and adorned as civilization advances, and may, so to speak, change its costume in accordance with the fashion of later times. . . . Many cases are known in which rude incidents have been dressed up in the chivalrous costume of later times. The French *Horn et Rimenhild*, e.g., represents the same story as the cruder English *King Horn*, only ' expanded by many courtly details of feast and tournament ' (Ward, *Catalogue of Romances*, I, 455)."

[2] *Romania*, XVII, 334–335 (1888).

l'époux, avec l'intention de revenir, et il oublie une promesse qu'il lui a donnée ou une défense qu'elle lui a faite ; l'anneau que la ‘ dame de la fontaine ’ (certainement une fée dans la version originaire) fait enlever à Ivain rappelle des incidents analogues de plusieurs contes qui ont la même donnée.   Ce nom de ‘ dame de la fontaine,’ devenu incompréhensible (cf. *Guingamor*, v. 122), a fait insérer ici l'histoire de la fontaine dont l'eau agitée provoque l'orage (croyance d'ailleurs celtique), et de la manière chevaleresque dont le héros s'en empare ; mais ces épisodes, pas plus que celui du lion reconnaissant, n'appartiennent au fonds primitif.''

In his smaller edition of *Yvain* in 1891 [1] Foerster replied to Paris by (1) stoutly asserting, without offering any proof, that *Laudine is not a fée*, and (2) by admitting that Chrétien may have borrowed the "forgotten promise" episode from some [*fée*] story like those mentioned by Paris : " Mag nun auch der Dichter wirklich das folgende (Vergessen des Versprechens) sich aus einem solchen Stoff geholt haben, sicher ist, dass die Episode, welche ich auf die Witwe von Ephesus zurückführte, damit unter keinen Umständen etwas zu thun hat." [2]

This passage contains a fatal admission of the true character of Foerster's method of dealing with literary origins.   He searches about for sources and finds one incident here and another there. Chrétien, he says, must have combined these various incidents.   To such a theory the addition of a few more entirely disconnected

---

[1] *Romanische Bibliothek*, V, xiv, footnote.

[2] In this same introduction to *Yvain* Foerster dwells particularly on his comparison of the Matron of Ephesus.   He says (p. xiii): " Diese leicht getröstete Witwe [Laudine] ist ein direkter Nachkomme der bekannten ‘ Witwe von Ephesus.’ Kein einziger aller der boshaften Züge, die das Original besitzt, fehlt dem neuen Abbild desselben."   The central point of the whole episode is, he thinks, indicated by the lines

> C'est cele qui prist
> Celui qui son seignor ocist (vv. 1809–10),

and this he regards as proved by the following reflection of the poet's :

> Mes or est mes sire Yvains sire,
> Et li morz est toz obliëz
> Cil qui l'ocist est mariëz
> An sa fame et ansanble gisent (vv. 2164 ff.).

sources can make little difference. A view like this cannot be refuted, just as it cannot be established. It can hold the field only in default of any explanation that shows, already combined, most of the elements which Foerster asks us to believe were brought together by Chrétien. The mosaic character of Foerster's theory is clearly shown by the analysis of Chrétien's *Ivain* which he has very recently published in his edition of the *Lancelot*[1]: "Ivain: örtliche Quellensage + Ring des Gyges + Wittwe von Ephesus + Löwe des Androklus." This, then, is the best outline Foerster is able to make of his theory, and it indicates four entirely disconnected sources. Moreover, there are, on his own admission, one or two other sources (e.g., for the Forgotten Promise and the Madness Motive) which he has simply omitted, not explained away.

Such a theory is manifestly unfair. Everybody knows that the most complicated story can be taken apart into simple elements, and these simple elements can then be found separately almost anywhere. It is not the finding of a single element that proves a source. The combination of elements alone is significant. The more elements already in combination a supposed source can show, the stronger, other things being equal, is the probability of its being the true one. These are the simplest principles of reasoning, but Foerster's method of dealing with this problem in literary origins seems to ignore them.

Of course this theory of Foerster's did not pass without challenge. In 1889 Mussafia[2] said: "So viel gestatte ich mir zu bemerken, dass ich die Ansicht, nach welcher das Motiv der leicht getrösteten Wittwe den eigentlichen Kern der Erzählung bilden soll, so bestechend sie auch erscheinen möge, als durchaus unhaltbar betrachte. Das wesentlichste Merkmal der weit verbreiteten Mähre bildet doch deren satirische Tendenz; sie will den Wankelmuth eines der sinnlichen Lust fröhnenden Weibes geisseln. Ein solcher Stoff lässt sich nicht veredeln und vertiefen, ohne dass er seine Existenzberechtigung einbüsse; Chrestien, welcher die Liebenden der Vergangenheit im Gegensatze zur Entartung der Zeitgenossen preist, kann doch nicht

---

[1] Christian von Troyes, *Sämtliche erhaltene Werke*, IV, lxxxi (1899), *Der Karrenritter und das Wilhelmsleben.*

[2] A. Mussafia, *Literaturblatt f. germ. u. rom. Phil.*, 1889, col. 221.

eine solche Untreue an dem heimgegangenen Gemahle als den eigentlichen Vorwurf seiner Dichtung gewählt haben."

Similarly, in 1890, Muret[1] remarked with reference to Foerster's
theory that the *Chevalier au Lion* is only a variant of the story of the
Matron of Ephesus: "A ce point de vue, le noyau du récit serait
formé par les trois ou quatre cents vers où Laudine, pressée par les
arguments de Lunète, se décide à épouser le meurtrier de son mari
bien-aimé.   La fontaine enchantée de la forêt de Brocéliande, Arthur
et sa cour, les aventures du chevalier Ivain — presque toute la nar-
ration en un mot, — ne fourniraient que des accessoires, habilement
disposés pour charmer un public engoué des héros de la Table-
Ronde.   Il est certain que la plupart des épisodes ne convergent
nullement autour du prétendu centre du poème.   Comme celui-ci
compte près de sept mille vers, on s'attendrait à ce que M. F. le
jugeât un des ouvrages les plus mal composés qu'il y ait dans aucune
littérature.   Nous sommes donc un peu surpris de lire, en tête de la
présente édition [1887] du *Chevalier au Lion*, que ce roman repré-
sente l'art d'un Chrétien de Troyes parvenu à son plus haut point
de perfection."

Finally, in 1896, Ahlström[2] replied to Foerster's arguments at
length: " M. Foerster affirme d'abord que notre roman est le seul où
Chrétien ne donne aucune indication sur l'origine du sujet.   Cela
prouve — selon M. Foerster — que l'auteur doit avoir eu une raison
toute spéciale pour garder le silence, résidant dans ce fait que l'auteur
ne devait sa matière à aucun livre ni à aucun conte, mais seulement
à sa propre imagination.

" La vérité des prémisses est au moins bien douteuse ; la conclusion
semble l'être encore plus.

" D'abord, on ne peut pas dire qu'il manque à notre roman toute
mention d'origine.   M. Holland a déjà attiré l'attention sur les vers
6816 et suiv.[3] . . . :

---

[1] Ernest Muret, *Revue Critique*, XXIX, 67 (1890).

[2] Axel Ahlström, *Sur l'Origine du Chevalier au Lion*, in *Mélanges dédiés à Carl Wahlund*, Mâcon, 1896, pp. 289–303.

[3] Ahlström quotes also vv. 33 ff., but I have omitted them, for it seems clear, as Paris pointed out in 1897 (*Romania*, XXVI, 106), that they are not in particular about Ivain, "mais en général d'Arthur."

v. 6814 Del *Chevalier au lion* fine
    Crestiiens son romanz einsi;
    Qu'onques plus conter n'an oï
    Ne ja plus n'an orroiz conter
    S'an n'i viaut mançonge ajoster.

"Il nous semble que dans ces quelques vers l'auteur se prononce assez positivement sur l'origine de son thème. Il l'a entendu conter. ... A notre avis, cela doit indiquer que Chrétien a rimé son roman d'après un conte en ce temps populaire chez les Bretons. ...

"Nous croyons donc que le poète a voulu lui-même indiquer un conte français ou breton comme ayant été la base de son roman; quand même il aurait gardé un silence complet, une conclusion comme celle de M. Foerster resterait toujours très incertaine" (pp. 290–291).

Ahlström then quotes Foerster's explanation of the story as a development from the theme of the Easily Consoled Widow, and adds: "En lisant ces lignes, ne croirait-on pas que la fameuse veuve d'Éphèse ait, elle aussi, commencé par maudire le meurtrier de son mari, qu'elle ait grondé sa pauvre suivante et que peu à peu elle ait changé d'avis pour finir par épouser le meurtrier?" On the contrary, as Ahlström points out, *there is in the Matron of Ephesus no marrying of the murderer of the husband.*

"D'un autre côté M. Foerster dit en propres termes qu'il ne manque à la copie aucun des vilains traits de l'original. Où M. Foerster trouve t-il donc dans le poème de Chrétien le trait le plus fameux et le plus affreux du conte: l'attentat de la veuve contre les restes de son mari?[1] ... Il n'existe, en vérité, aucune de ces infamies

---

[1] Ahlström brings forward several other traits of the mediæval *Matron of Ephesus* story which separate it entirely from that of Laudine. I have omitted these points because Paris, who entirely agrees as to the vast chasm that separates any forms of the two stories, admits that Ahlström "n'aurait pas dû citer, comme les plus connus et les plus essentiels, des traits qui ne sont ni dans Phèdre ni dans Pétrone et n'appartiennent qu'aux rédactions médiévales contenues dans le roman des *Sept Sages*" (*Romania*, XXVI, 106). For references to various forms of the story, see Keller, *Li Romans des Sept Sages*, 1836, pp. clix ff.; Grisebach, *Die Wanderung der Novelle von der treulosen Wittwe durch die Weltlitteratur*, Berlin, 1886 (2d ed., 1889); Cesari, *Come pervenne e rimase in Italia la Matrona d'Efeso*, Bologna, 1890.

dans le beau roman de Chrétien.   La dame de la fontaine pleure
sincèrement son époux et honore son corps et sa mémoire.

"Mais, dit à la fin M. Foerster, celui qui n'est pas encore con-
vaincu le sera sans doute par les mots que le poète lui-même a mis
dans la bouche de la veuve :

> v. 1809   C'est cele qui prist
> Celui qui son seignor ocist,"

which the poet repeats in v. 2166.

"Selon notre opinion, le poète accentue dans ces lignes précisé-
ment et exclusivement un des points dans lesquels le roman s'éloigne
le plus du conte, savoir ce fait que la veuve du roman épouse le
meurtrier de son mari.   Il est donc peut-être un peu hardi de vouloir
ainsi prouver la relation intime entre les deux sujets.

"La ressemblance entre le roman et le conte se borne, en effet, à
ce point commun qu'une veuve désolée change de sentiments en peu
de temps et veut se remarier.   Tous les détails sont différents.   Il y
a pourtant, dans la littérature comme dans la vie, trop de jeunes
veuves qui désirent se remarier le plus tôt possible, pour que ce fait
seul puisse prouver l'existence d'un rapport plus intime entre le conte
et le roman."

Up to the present time, then, a violent controversy has raged about
the *Matron of Ephesus* theory, in which, on the whole, it has been
rather badly damaged.   It will be the purpose of the next chapter
to examine the question afresh.

CHAPTER II.

THE *MATRON OF EPHESUS* AND CHRÉTIEN'S *IVAIN*.

In order to bring out as fairly as possible the fatal difficulties that
stand in the way of Foerster's hypothesis, it will be necessary to
quote in full the story to which he refers and to follow it with a
tolerably complete summary of Chrétien's *Ivain*.

The version of the *Matron of Ephesus* given by Petronius is longer than that of Phædrus [1] and more favorable than any other to Foerster's hypothesis. It is therefore the one here selected.

THE MATRON OF EPHESUS. [2]

Matrona quaedam Ephesi tam notae erat pudicitiae, ut vicinarum quoque gentium feminas ad spectaculum sui evocaret. Haec ergo cum virum extulisset, non contenta vulgari more funus passis prosequi crinibus aut nudatum pectus in conspectu frequentiae plangere, in conditorium etiam prosecuta est defunctum, positumque in hypogaeo Graeco more corpus custodire ac flere totis noctibus diebusque coepit. Sic afflictantem se ac mortem inedia persequentem non parentes potuerunt abducere, non propinqui; magistratus ultimo repulsi abierunt complocrataque singularis exempli femina ab omnibus quintum iam diem sine alimento trahebat. Assidebat aegrae fidissima ancilla, simulque et lacrimas commodabat lugenti, et quotienscunque defecerat positum in monumento lumen renovabat. Una igitur in tota civitate fabula erat, solum illud affulsisse verum pudicitiae amorisque exemplum omnis ordinis homines confitebantur, cum interim imperator provinciae latrones iussit crucibus affigi secundum illam casulam, in qua recens cadaver matrona deflebat. Proxima ergo nocte, cum miles, qui cruces asservabat, ne quis ad sepulturam corpus detraheret, notasset sibi [et] lumen inter monumenta clarius fulgens et gemitum lugentis audisset, vitio gentis humanae concupiit scire, quis aut quid faceret. Descendit igitur in conditorium, visaque pulcherrima muliere primo quasi quodam monstro infernisque imaginibus turbatus substitit. Deinde ut et corpus iacentis conspexit et lacrimas consideravit faciemque unguibus sectam, ratus scilicet id quod erat, desiderium extincti non posse feminam pati, attulit in monumentum cenulam suam coepitque hortari lugentem, ne perseveraret in dolore supervacuo ac nihil profuturo gemitu pectus diduceret: omnium eundem esse exitum [sed] et idem domicilium, et cetera quibus exulceratae mentes ad sanitatem revocantur. At illa ignota consolatione percussa laceravit vehementius pectus ruptosque crines super corpus iacentis imposuit. Non recessit tamen miles, sed eadem exhortatione temptavit

---

[1] For the story in Phædrus, see Hervieux, *Les Fabulistes Latins*, II, *Phèdre et ses Anciens Imitateurs*, Paris, 1884, pp. 66–67 (2d ed., 1894, pp. 72–73). See also p. 269 (2d ed., pp. 340–341).

[2] Petronius, *Satirae*, Buecheler's 3d ed., Berlin, 1882, chaps. 111, 112, pp. 77–78.

dare mulierculae cibum, donec ancilla vini certe ab eo odore corrupta
primum ipsa porrexit ad humanitatem invitantis victam
manum, deinde refecta potione et cibo expugnare dominae
pertinaciam coepit et "quid proderit" inquit "hoc tibi, si
soluta inedia fueris, si te vivam sepelieris, si antequam fata
poscant, indemnatum spiritum effuderis?

The Lady's Maid takes the Soldier's Part.

id cinerem aut manes credis sentire sepultos?
vis tu reviviscere? vis discusso muliebri errore, quam diu licuerit, lucis commodis frui? ipsum te iacentis corpus admonere debet, ut vivas." Nemo
invitus audit, cum cogitur aut cibum sumere aut vivere. Itaque mulier
aliquot dierum abstinentia sicca passa est frangi pertinaciam suam, nec
minus avide replevit se cibo quam ancilla, quae prior victa est. Ceterum
scitis, quid plerumque soleat temptare humanam satietatem.
Quibus blanditiis impetraverat miles, ut matrona vellet vivere,
isdem etiam pudicitiam eius aggressus est. Nec deformis aut infacundus iuvenis castae videbatur, conciliante
gratiam ancilla ac subinde dicente:

The newly Bereaved Widow remarries suddenly.

"placitone etiam pugnabis amori?
Nec venit in mentem, quorum consederis arvis?"

Quid diutius moror? Ne hanc quidem partem corporis mulier abstinuit,
victorque miles utrumque persuasit. Iacuerunt ergo una non tantum illa
nocte, qua nuptias fecerunt, sed postero etiam ac tertio die, praeclusis
videlicet conditorii foribus, ut quisquis ex notis ignotisque ad monumentum
venisset, putaret expirasse super corpus viri pudicissimam uxorem. Ceterum
delectatus miles et forma mulieris et secreto, quicquid boni per facultates
poterat, coemebat et prima statim nocte in monumentum ferebat. Itaque
unius cruciarii parentes ut viderunt laxatam custodiam, detraxere nocte
pendentem supremoque mandaverunt officio. At miles circumscriptus dum
desidet, ut postero die vidit unam sine cadavere crucem, veritus supplicium,
mulieri quid accidisset exponit: nec se expectaturum iudicis sententiam,
sed gladio ius dicturum ignaviae suae. Commodaret ergo illa perituro
locum et fatale conditorium familiari ac viro faceret. Mulier non minus
misericors quam pudica "ne istud" inquit "dii sinant, ut eodem tempore
duorum mihi carissimorum hominum duo funera spectem. Malo mortuum
impendere quam vivum occidere." Secundum hanc orationem iubet ex
arca corpus mariti sui tolli atque illi, quae vacabat, cruci affigi. Usus est
miles ingenio prudentissimae feminae, posteroque die populus miratus est,
qua ratione mortuus isset in crucem.

THE *IVAIN* OF CHRÉTIEN DE TROIES.[1]

I. The story opens at Carduel in Wales, where Arthur is holding

The Tale of a Previous Adventurer.

court. King Arthur and the queen have withdrawn to their chamber, and Calogrenant has begun a tale to the assembled knights, of whom Iwain is one. The queen enters to hear it also, and he begins again at her request (vv. 1–174).

II. "About seven years ago," says Calogrenant, "I wandered all day through the Forest of Broceliande till I came to a strongly

The Hospitable Host.

fortified place. The lord of the *forteresse* gave me a splendid welcome, and a fair maid disarmed me and entertained me in a meadow till supper. The supper was entirely to my taste because of the maid who sat opposite to me. I spent a pleasant night in that castle" (vv. 175–269).

III. "In the morning I set out, and not far off I found fierce bulls fighting and a black creature with a head larger than a horse's,

The Giant Herdsman.

armed with a club, guarding them. Finding that this creature could speak, I asked him to direct me to some adventure. He showed me the path to a fountain [the Fountain Perilous], telling me also what I might do" (vv. 270–409).

IV. "I reached the Fountain about noon. By it stood the

Marvellous Landscape.

most beautiful tree that ever grew on earth. I took a basin of gold that was attached by a chain to the tree, and, dipping up some water, I poured it on the rock" (vv. 410–438).

V. "Forthwith there ensued a terrible storm of wind and rain; then a calm in which the birds sang sweetly on the tree. After

The Rain-Making Fountain.

this there appeared a knight on horseback, who attacked and overthrew me. I came home on foot like a fool and like a fool have told my story."

During the talk that follows, Arthur comes out of his chamber, hears the story repeated, and declares that he will go with his knights within a fortnight, namely just before St. John the Baptist's Day, to essay the adventure. Iwain, however, is anxious to try it alone; so

---

[1] Summarized from Foerster's *Yvain, Romanische Bibliothek,* V.

he steals away secretly.   He is entertained at night by the Hospitable Host; next morning he sees the Giant Herdsman, and he comes at last to the Fountain Perilous.   He pours water on the rock.   The storm follows (vv. 439–810).

VI. After this the armed knight appears and attacks Iwain. They fight till Iwain deals the knight a blow that cleaves his helmet
The Combat. and wounds him in the brain.   The knight flees, pursued by Iwain, through the streets of a town and up to the gate of a palace (vv. 811–906).

VII. The knight rides under a sharp iron gate, which is arranged to drop like the fall of a rat trap if one touches the spring.   Iwain
The Falling follows hard after, and his horse accidentally touches
Gates. the spring.   The gate falls close behind Iwain and with its knife edge cuts his horse in two, cutting off the hinder part of the saddle and also the rider's spurs.   Another gate at the same time descends in front, and Iwain is imprisoned in a *sale* (vv. 907–969).

VIII. But a damsel, called Lunete, issues from a narrow door and recognizes him as Iwain, son of King Urien.   She was once sent on
Protection a message by her lady to King Arthur's court, and,
by the perhaps because she was not so courteous as a damsel
Lady's Confidante. ought to be, no knight deigned to speak to her except Iwain.   He honored and served her, and she is glad to recompense him now (vv. 970–1019).

IX. She gives Iwain a magic ring that, when the stone set in it is
Invisible-Render- enclosed in the hand, makes its wearer invisible, and
ing Ring. she brings him food to eat (vv. 1020–1054).

X. Presently men come with clubs and swords, seeking him who slew their lord, Esclados le Ros.   They do not find Iwain, for the
It was the Lady's ring renders him invisible.   Lunete's mistress, whose
Husband that the name is Laudine, a most beautiful lady, now enters,
Hero has killed. weeping for her lord, who is carried on a bier (1055–1172).

XI. When the corpse is brought into the hall where Iwain is,
The Corpse bleeds it begins to bleed.   The men feel confident that the
before the Slayer. murderer must be hidden there, and they renew their search (vv. 1173–1242).

XII. When Iwain sees Laudine, he is smitten with violent love for her. He even watches the funeral, so as to catch a better glimpse of her. He refuses to go when Lunete offers to help him to escape. Effects of the Lunete persuades her lady that she ought to feel no Lady's Beauty. hatred against the knight who slew her husband. She reminds her that the Dameisele Sauvage has sent word that King Arthur is coming within a week to essay the Fountain. Laudine feels that a knight is needed to defend it. Lunete tells her that the knight who slew her husband would undertake to do it. When Laudine learns that his name is Iwain she consents (vv. 1243–1942).

XIII. Iwain is terrified when ushered into Laudine's presence and says that anything she may lay upon him, even death, he will Marriage with take without ill will. She receives him kindly when the Lady. he promises to defend the Fountain. Iwain and the lady are speedily married, and there is great joy (vv. 1943–2169).

XIV. The wedding feast lasts till King Arthur comes to essay the adventure of the Fountain. Kay is assigned to the adventure. The Arrival of king pours water on the rock, and presently Iwain King Arthur. appears mounted on a powerful horse and overthrows Kay. Iwain then reveals himself to Arthur and escorts him and his knights to the castle, where they are entertained for a week (vv. 2170–2475).

XV. When Arthur departs, Iwain is persuaded to accompany him. Laudine does not give Iwain permission to go till he has promised Departure of to return within a year. If he does not come back Iwain. by that time, "her love will turn to hate." She gives Iwain a ring that will protect him from imprisonment and be his shield and hauberk (vv. 2476–2638).

XVI. A year has passed, and Iwain is busy in tournaments. Suddenly he recollects that he has overstayed his time. The same Broken Promise instant a damsel rides up and calls him a hypocrite, and Madness. and a thief who has stolen her lady's heart and forgotten his promise to return. She demands back the ring. When Iwain does not reply, she snatches the ring from his finger and departs. Iwain goes mad and runs into the forest, where he lives like a beast. A hermit supplies him with musty bread (vv. 2639–2884).

XVII. At length one day a lady, accompanied by two damsels, finds a naked man asleep in the forest. One of the damsels recog-

Cure by a
Magic Remedy.

nizes Iwain by a scar on his cheek. At her request the lady allows the damsel to bring a box of ointment, a gift from Morgue the Wise,[1] by means of which Iwain is cured of his madness. In return Iwain frees the lady from the oppression of a powerful enemy, Count Alier (vv. 2885–3340).

XVIII. As Iwain is riding through a deep forest, he finds a serpent and a lion fighting. He succors the lion and slays the serpent. The lion kneels down before Iwain and indicates by his

The Thankful
Lion.

tears that he thanks him. After this the lion accompanies Iwain everywhere. Iwain comes to the Fountain Perilous and finds Lunete shut up in the little chapel near by. She tells Iwain a wicked seneschal has accused her of treason in persuading Laudine to marry Iwain. She is to be burned to-morrow unless a knight can be found who will fight the seneschal and two others, in order to prove her innocence. Iwain promises to undertake the combat but is obliged to go some distance before he finds lodgings for the night at a castle (vv. 3341–3816).

XIX. This castle is beset by a giant, Harpin of the Mountain, who will kill the lord's sons or carry off the daughter of the house

Conflicting
Appointments.

in the morning unless a champion can be found to fight him. Iwain promises to fight the giant if the latter appears early in the morning; otherwise he shall be obliged to go to keep his promise and save Lunete (vv. 3817–4087).

XX. In the morning Iwain waits till prime for the giant to appear,

Combat with
Giant Harpin.

and, as he does not come, is distracted in his mind whether to go or stay. At last Harpin comes and Iwain subdues him, aided in the struggle by his faithful lion (vv. 4088–4312).

XXI. Iwain rides hurriedly to the Fountain Perilous, and arrives

The Rescue of a
Damsel by a
Judicial Combat.

in time to rescue Lunete by fighting at once the wicked seneschal and two others. The lion again helps Iwain. Laudine does not know who Iwain is. He calls himself the Knight of the Lion (vv. 4313–4702).

---

[1] That is, Morgain la fée.

XXII. Iwain is met by a messenger from the younger daughter of the lord of La Noire Espine. The lord is dead, and the elder Daughters of the Black Thorn. daughter has usurped all the land and secured Gawain to defend her claim. Iwain, who does not know that his opponent will be Gawain, agrees to fight for the younger daughter. He does not reveal his own name but is called the Knight of the Lion (vv. 4703–5106).

XXIII. Iwain and the messenger come to a place called the Castle of Ill Adventure and are advised not to enter. They do enter, however, and find three hundred girls behind a row of stakes. The Castle of Ill Adventure. These girls are pale and thin and obliged to toil at working silk with thread of gold. It is explained that many years ago the King of the Isle of Maidens went like a fool in search of adventure. He fell into the power of two " fiz de deable " who own this castle. Being not yet eighteen years old, he ransomed himself as best he could by swearing to send each year thirty maidens as tribute till the monsters should be vanquished. Iwain is well entertained for the night by the lord and lady of the castle, but in the morning he is obliged to fight the monsters. He overcomes them, with the aid of his lion, and frees the maidens (vv. 5107–5811).

XXIV. Iwain arrives at Arthur's court clad in armor and known as the Knight of the Lion. Gawain, too, is disguised by his armor, Combat of Fratres Jurati. and the two friends fight a terrible battle. When night comes on, they grow tired, and reveal themselves to each other. There is great joy, and people are surprised to see how evenly they are matched (vv. 5812–6526).

XXV. Iwain soon returns to the Fountain Perilous and stirs up Reconciliation between the Hero and the Heroine. such a storm that the castle is almost destroyed. Lunete is sent to find out who is at the Fountain, and by her mediation Iwain is reconciled to Laudine. Now Iwain has peace and through joy the past is forgotten (vv. 6527–6818).

Every reader who compares the *Ivain* with the *Matron of Ephesus* will at once observe that they belong to two entirely different kinds of writing. Chrétien's *Ivain* is romantic in the highest degree. It is far removed even from realistic literature, and much more from that class of disillusioned, cynical stories to which the *Matron of*

Ephesus so evidently belongs.[1] The strongest proofs in the world
would barely suffice to make one believe that Chrétien drew the
theme of his curiously high-spirited, un-matter-of-fact romance from
a cheap satire on women.

But what *are* the proofs?   Merely similarities of incident.   Historical evidence is of course unobtainable.   Now there are but two
incidents in the two stories that are similar.   The first is, that in
both there is a lady's maid who takes the hero's part.   Surely not
much can be based on this.   Every lady has a maid, and from time
immemorial approach to a lady has been by means of her maid.
The other incident, upon which so much stress has been laid, is, not
that in both stories the widow marries the slayer of her husband, —
a parallel that might have some significance, — but simply that in
both stories a newly bereaved widow marries again suddenly.   As
Ahlström has well said, it is not necessary to go to the *Matron of
Ephesus* for this.   The incident is not unknown in real life.   One
should also remember that in the Middle Ages every widow left in
possession of a fief was practically forced to marry again to protect
her possessions.   Such a marriage might follow the death of the
widow's husband almost immediately if there was danger of invasion
or attack.

Some one may remind me that it has been urged also that a similarity lies in the heartlessness of the lady's treatment of her husband
in both stories.   This is the weakest point of all.   Laudine is not
described by Chrétien as heartless.   So far as can be made out, he
represents her as respecting her husband's memory to the last.

Furthermore, stretch the *Matron of Ephesus* theory to its greatest
conceivable limits, it still will not account for more than five or six
hundred lines out of the almost seven thousand of the *Ivain*.   The
remainder of the romance would have to be explained as a mere
compilation from various disconnected sources.   Even, therefore, if

---

[1] The cynical side of the *Matron of Ephesus* is brought out in a still more
repellent way in the mediæval versions of the tale, which Chrétien would naturally
have known.   In them the widow with her own hands mutilates the body of her
husband to make it resemble the stolen corpse, which had lost its ears and some
teeth.

there were no other theory in the field, it would seem as if the hypothesis which derives the plot from the *Matron of Ephesus* would have to be rejected. It has, so far as I can see, not a leg to stand on.

CHAPTER III.

HISTORY OF THE CELTIC THEORY.

THE view which would explain the *Ivain* as in origin a Celtic story of a "fairy mistress" was first distinctly set forth by Alfred Nutt in 1887.[1] "The Lady of the Fountain seems to me to be an expansion of a Goldenlocks story. The hero leaves his wife (breaking a taboo thereby), is forsaken of her, becomes rough and hairy, rescues her from three successive dangers, is recognized by and reunited to her. It is to be noted that the hero is accompanied by a helping animal. The opening incident of this story may be compared to Joyce's Pursuit of the Gilla Dacker [i.e. the story of Diarmat].[2] . . . In both stories the heroes drink of the fountain, the lord of the fountain appears, and a fight ensues in which the hero proves victor."

This view was expressed by Paris in his usual felicitous way in the passage already quoted[3] from *Romania*, 1888. It is also the view of Muret, set forth in 1890 in the article from which a quotation has

---

[1] *The Celtic Magazine*, XII, 555. Osterwald, *Iwein, ein keltischer Frühlingsgott*, 1853, pointed out that Laudine is an other-world person, and that this is the clue to her sudden marriage to the slayer of her husband. His article, however, is overlaid with vague mythologizing. The remark of Alexander Macbain in 1884 should also be noted: "Visits of the nature of that undertaken by Ulysses, in Homer, to the Land of the Shades, were made by at least three champions of the Gael, . . . Cuchulainn, Cormac and Diarmat. . . . We find a double account of Diarmat's visit to *Tir-fa-tonn*, one Irish, one Gaelic. The Irish one is in its main features the counterpart of the Welsh Mabinogion, 'The Lady of the Fountain'" (*Celtic Magazine*, IX, 278).

[2] Rhŷs (*Lectures on Celtic Heathendom*, London, 1888, pp. 187 ff.) has made this same comparison, and so has Ferdinand Lot (*Romania*, XXI, 67–71).

[3] Pp. 5–6, above.

already been made.[1]   He thinks that it is clear to any unprejudiced person that the principal *donnée* of the *Chevalier au Lion* is one of those stories of a mortal loved by a *fée* so common in popular tradition.   He points to the existence of analogous situations in many of those *lais bretons* of which nobody disputes the Celtic origin, and concludes : " A des yeux non prévenus, les circonstances singulières du mariage d'Ivain avec la *Dame de la Fontaine* n'ont que le plus vague et le plus lointain rapport avec l'anecdote de la Matrone d'Éphèse."   Muret thinks that Chrétien's original was probably some prose recital he had heard, though he admits that a few " aventures banales " may be of the poet's own introduction.

Ahlström, who expresses himself at some length in the article already referred to,[2] agrees that the original of the *Ivain* story is the well-known account of the union of a mortal to a supernatural being, whether, as in *Cupid and Psyche*, the hero is supernatural, or as in *Graelent, Lanval, Guingamor, Guigemar, Désiré, Partenopeus de Blois, Floriant et Florete, Bel Inconnu, La Châtelaine de Vergi, Perceval* (several times), *Erec, Lancelot*, and *Ogier le Danois*, it is the heroine who is a *fée*.   In one or two of these stories, as Ahlström thinks, the *fée* was originally a swan-maiden caught by stealing the swan-raiment which she had temporarily laid aside while bathing in a fountain. It is certainly true that in *Graelent* and *Guingamor* swan-maiden features have been mixed up with the story, for in both the hero obtains the love of the lady, surprised while bathing in a fountain, by possessing himself of her clothes.   In neither case, however, has this confusion destroyed her real character as a *fée* princess.   In neither case, as Schofield has clearly pointed out,[3] is the heroine like the maiden in *Dolopathos* (which he shows to be a genuine swan-maiden story) " a weak, defenceless captive."   She is " a queenly princess.   She does not humbly accept a marriage forced upon her, but comes from a distant land solely to carry back the hero whom

---

[1] *Revue Critique*, XXIX, 67.

[2] *Mélanges Wahlund*, 1896, pp. 294–303.

[3] See his important articles, *The Lay of Guingamor*, in *Harvard Studies and Notes*, V, 236 ff., and *The Lays of Graelent and Lanval*, in *Publ. of the Mod. Lang. Association of America*, XV, 145.

she loves,—not in the future to be a wife patiently enduring all
sorts of indignities, but a proud supernatural mistress whose commands when not followed to the letter bring sorrow to him whose
life even is in her hands." [1] In both cases she speaks her mind with
dignity and is not really surprised, while a swan-maiden is always
taken unawares. Dr. Schofield's view that these heroines are true
fées to whom the authors, confused by the resemblances of their
stories to tales like that in the *Dolopathos*, have ascribed certain
swan-maiden features, is altogether the most reasonable. Ahlström,
however, holds the opposite opinion, that the swan character of the
lady was original and has been modified by stories of *fées*. He also
maintains that *Désiré*, where it is the lady's maid that is caught at
the fountain, and *Lanval*, where two maids are met while carrying
water to their mistress, are in origin swan-maiden stories which have
lost most of their primitive character. Not content with this, he
goes on to draw the unwarranted inference that *Ivain* is another
such swan-maiden story. He admits that no trace of this supposed
origin can be found except the name "Lady of the Fountain," but
this single hint is enough, he thinks, to enable him to reconstruct
the whole.

The weakness of Ahlström's argument becomes apparent when
one reflects that it would prove practically all fairy mistresses to be
swan-maidens. They are nearly all first seen near a spring or river
or lake or by the seaside. Especially is this the case in Celtic
fairy stories, because of the belief, strongly held by the Celts, that
the approach to fairyland lay across the sea or beneath the waves.
There are plenty of ways in which a fairy might come to be called a
lady of the fountain without her having been in origin a swan-maiden
at all. Nor is this swan-maiden feature at all necessary to the rest
of Ahlström's explanation.

Ahlström's confusion of *fées* with swan-maidens leads him to explain
that Laudine's sudden remarriage is due to her *fairy* nature,[2] which
(he seems to think) places her at the *disposal* of the conqueror of
the Fountain. Any one who studies the Celtic *fée*, however, will see

---

[1] Schofield, l.c., p. 236.
[2] See *Mélanges-Wahlund*, pp. 296–297.

that she was originally bound by no restrictions and at nobody's *disposal.* (The sudden remarriage is really due to the fact that the slain warrior was originally a supernatural being in the service of the *fée*, and not her husband at all.) Ahlström, with some probability, explains the ring given to Iwain as originally the ring that brought the fairy mistress at any time and place, while she remained invisible to every one but the hero. It is easy to see how this might get changed to a ring that renders its wearer invisible. Its being taken away when Ivain is unfaithful is paralleled in *Désiré.* It would be absurd, therefore, to regard it as an adaptation of the ring of Gyges.[1]

Ahlström's most interesting suggestion is that the Joy of the Court episode in *Erec* is really a defective version of the fairy mistress story. As *Erec* was written before *Ivain*, it becomes clear that a fairy mistress story in which the knight was obliged to do battle with all who approached his lady existed before *Ivain* was written. Chrétien's original, then, must have been a story of some length, comprising at least three of the chief incidents of the poem: the fight at the fountain, the remarriage, and the thankful lion.[2] This story, he believes, came from Brittany, where it had been localized. " C'est donc, si l'on veut, un sujet breton ; mais on ne peut dire qu'il soit né dans ce pays ni que le poète l'ait directement emprunté des Bretons" (p. 303).

In 1897 Baist,[3] in a short but important note, discussed the whole question of the sources of *Ivain*. With regard to Ahlström's swan-maiden explanation he says: "Ich bin von jeher der Meinung gewesen, dass in Laudine sich eine Wasserfrau verberge." He naturally, however, fails to see that she can be made such a water-nymph, simply because she happens to be a *fée*. Baist divides the romance of *Ivain*

---

[1] Ahlström believes also that he has found a parallel to the madness of Ivain in *Lanval*, v. 416: " Mult dotouent qu'il s'afolast"; but Paris and Tobler more properly translate this by "do injury to himself" (*Romania*, XXVI, 107; *Zt. f. rom. Phil.*, X, 168).

[2] Ahlström regards the episode of the thankful lion as an invention to explain the title " Chevalier au Lion," which he, without good reason, thinks came in the first place from the name of a country, *Léonnois* (pp. 299–300).

[3] *Zt. f. rom. Phil.*, XXI, 402–405.

into two parts. The second part, beginning immediately after the hero loses Laudine, he believes to be Chrétien's own invention or compilation. The madness of Ivain is, he thinks, borrowed from that of Tristan. (But surely this must have been a part of the original fairy mistress story, of which it is a well-recognized feature.) The introduction of the thankful lion he with much reason ascribes to Chrétien. He points out that the interest centres in this brilliant piece of decoration up to the time of the combat of Iwain and Gawain. None of the adventures related in this second part could belong, he thinks, to an original Journey of Wonders that led the hero back to his fairy mistress, except that of the Castle of the Black Thorn, and that shows no evidence of having belonged to such a tale. The Maiden Castle comes from some *Märchen.* The reconciliation at the end is, according to Baist, entirely the invention of Chrétien, because it is only a variant of the way in which the lady was at first persuaded by Lunete to receive the hero. (Yet Baist could hardly deny that a happy ending, though not perhaps a feature of the most primitive form of the theme, might easily have become attached to it long before it reached Chrétien.)

The first part of the romance Baist ascribes to "ein genau lokalisiertes bretonisches Märchen." He finds in it, to be sure, a verbal borrowing from Wace :

> Einsi alai, einsi reving,
> Au revenir por fol me ting.
> Si vos ai conté come fos
> Ce qu'onques mes conter ne vos. — YVAIN (vv. 577 ff.).

> Fol m'en reuinc, fol i alai,
> Fol i alai, fol m'en reuinc,
> Folie quis, por fol me tinc. — ROMAN DE ROU (vv. 6418 ff.).

This parallel might at first make one think that Chrétien developed his story of the Fountain out of the hint given in the *Roman de Rou*, but Baist shows that this cannot be, for the Giant Herdsman who points out the way is plainly "eine märchenhafte Gestalt" whose invention is not to be ascribed to Chrétien. There remains, however, the possibility that Chrétien transferred a story about some Magic Fountain to the particular Fountain of Barenton of which he learned from the poem of Wace.[1] That this part of the *Ivain* is based on a popular tale is proved, Baist thinks, by the repeated pointing out of the way, both at the Hospitable Castle and by the Giant Herdsman, by the contrasting of a first adventurer who fails with a second who succeeds, and by the repetition in both cases of the various particulars, all of which is " ganz genau im Märchenstil." One may guess, says Baist, that originally the Hospitable Castle and the Giant Herdsman " stood in more intimate relations with the adventure than Chrétien has cared to preserve." The change which Chrétien has made from the stags and hawks mentioned by Wace [2] to a herd of wild cattle, Baist believes to be significant, for marvellous herdsmen are common in insular Celtic stories. They are generally giant swineherds, but in the *Voyage of Maelduin* [3] there is a gigantic cattle driver who points out the way. The figure, Baist thinks, is surely traditional. Finally, Baist declares that to the Welsh it was a matter of course that the Fairy of the Fountain belonged to the Winner of the Fountain. The French did not understand this, and so Chrétien introduced out of his own head the long psychological discussion by which Laudine is persuaded to marry the conqueror. To the Welsh the lady was a mere prize.[4]

---

[1] It seems more probable that the Other-World fountain had been already localized at Barenton before the time of Chrétien and Wace.

[2] *Roman de Rou*, 6409 ff. (ed. H. Andresen, II, 284):

> La [Barenton] seut l'en les fees ueeir,
> Se li Breton nos dient ueir,
> E altres merueilles plusors;
> Aires i selt aueir *d'ostors*
> *E de granz cers mult grant plente;*
> Mais vilain ont tot deserte.
> La alai io merueilles querre,
> Vi la forest e ui la terre,
> Merueilles quis, mais nes trouai.

Then follow the three lines just quoted (p. 23).

[3] D'Arbois de Jubainville, *Cours de Litt. Celtique*, V, 472.

[4] Baist compares *Kulhwch and Olwen* (J. Loth, *Les Mabinogion*, I, 188–189), in which Kilydd asks where he shall find a wife: " ' I know one who will please you,' said one of his counsellors, ' that is the wife of King Doget,' and they resolved to fetch her, slew the king and carried away the lady." In the next sentence she is the wife of Kilydd. That she has become so the narrative does not think it

A brief but powerful statement of the view whose development has just been sketched, and one that may be appropriately quoted in conclusion, was published by Kittredge in 1898.[1] " The *Cligés*, we may remark in passing, formed no original part of 'the matter of Britain'; its Arthurian relations are due entirely to Chrétien. On this point there is no controversy. If now the ' Cligés' be compared with those works of the same author which are commonly thought to be referable to Celtic sources, the essential difference will be found striking, and in our opinion, significant.[2] . . . In the *Knight of the Lion* we have an admirable specimen of what one means by a 'romance of the Round Table.' . . . The lady is of course a *fée*, whose fate it is to marry whoever can overcome the (eldritch) knight who guards the well in the forest. But her husband can retain her favor only on terms of obedience and fidelity. Just as actual unfaithfulness to a fairy wife or fairy mistress always brings disaster and sometimes death, so, in this softened and rationalized form of the tale, the forgetfulness of Iwain and his failure to keep his day come near costing him the love of his lady. Her implacability is originally an essential trait of her fairy nature, though Chrétien himself may not have understood it in this way or have been aware that she was a *fée* at all, any more than Shakspere fully understood the mythological antecedents of the Scandinavian Norns whom he found in Holinshed's account of Macbeth."

Every one, it will be observed, who has advocated what may be called the fairy mistress explanation of the romance of *Ivain*, has looked for a source in Celtic tradition. This is evidently the natural view. Chrétien practically tells us that he is following a *conte*, which he evidently expects us to regard as based on Celtic tradition ; nearly

---

necessary to mention. This parallel is of course interesting, but the real point is not the brutality of Welsh customs, but the fact that Laudine was a fairy, and not originally the wife of Esclados at all.

[1] In a book review in the New York *Nation*, Feb. 24, 1898, LXVI, 150–151.

[2] Important evidence for the theory of a different origin of the *Ivain* from that of the *Cligés* is here brought forward. No one can pass directly from the former to the latter without being struck by the absence of those peculiarly Celtic features of fairy, wild man, and magic forest which give a distinctive flavor to the *Chevalier au Lion*.

all the names of the *dramatis personae* are Celtic; and the scene is
laid in Wales or Armorica. There is, moreover, a special reason
why this antecedent probability that the story of *Ivain* comes from
Celtic sources is very great. The Celtic *fées* are distinctly superior
beings, never surprised and taken captive by the hero, as the Germanic
fairies regularly are, but dwelling like Laudine in a magic land,
which must be visited by the hero, who thus puts himself in their
power before his courtship even begins. They retain their superiority,
and, like Iwain's mistress, insist on being obeyed even in the verbal
details of a promise or else they punish and forsake their lover, who
is always thought of as in their power.[1]   Evidently it is from creatures
like these, as distinguished from Germanic and other fairies, that
such a character as Laudine must be derived.

---

[1] The important suggestion that the typical heroine of the French Arthurian
romances of the twelfth century, who is thought of as far above her lover or her
husband, was derived essentially from the ancient Celtic *fée* is due to Alfred Nutt
(*Studies on the Legend of the Holy Grail*, pp. 232 ff.). Nutt points out that in
Teutonic fairy stories the man plays the chief part, sometimes even forcing the
fairy maiden to become his mistress. It is otherwise with the Celts: "Connla
and Bran and Oisin must all leave this earth and sail across ocean or lake before
they can rejoin their lady love; even Cuchullain, mightiest of all the heroes, is
constrained, struggle as he may, to go and dwell with the fairy queen Fand, who has
wooed him. Throughout, the immortal mistress retains her superiority. . . . This
type of womanhood, capricious, independent, severed from ordinary domestic life,
is assuredly the original of the Viviens, the Orgueilleuses, the Ladies of the
Fountain of the romances; it is also one which must have commended itself to
knightly devotees of mediæval romantic love. Their '*dame d'amour*' was as a
rule another man's wife; she raised in their minds no thought of home or child.
In the tone of their feelings towards her . . . they were closer akin to Oisin and
Neave, to Cuchullain and Fand, than to Siegfried and Brunhild, or to Roland
and Aude." In a more recent publication (*Voyage of Bran*, I, 156, note) Nutt
has also said: "There is no parallel to the position or the sentiments of a
Celtic heroine like Fand in the post-classic literature of Western Europe before
Guinevere." (He might have said, before Laudine.)

CHAPTER IV.

ANCIENT CELTIC STORIES OF THE JOURNEY TO THE OTHER WORLD.

I. THE TYPE.

To reach any just conclusion with respect to the question of the dependence of Chrétien's *Ivain* on Celtic Other-World stories, it is indispensable to secure as clear a conception as possible of what a typical Celtic fairy mistress story really was. It is extremely important, therefore, to have before us, at least in outline, all significant tales of this character which are unmistakably attested, on manuscript or other evidence, as belonging to a period more ancient than that of Chrétien.

In the case of Irish materials the evidence is of the most satisfactory sort imaginable. All of the Irish stories that will be quoted or summarized in the text of this chapter are preserved, at least in part, in one of two ancient manuscripts, the *Lebor na h-Uidre* and the *Book of Leinster*, which were written before the period of the rise of French Arthurian romance. The *Lebor na h-Uidre* (LU) was compiled and transcribed about the year 1100 by Moelmuiri mac Ceileachair, who died in 1106.[1] The *Book of Leinster* (LL) is as old as the year 1150.[2] These two manuscripts have preserved a mass of Irish Other-World lore of greater proved antiquity and of a more distinctive character than the fairy tales of any other Western people.

In Welsh, as in most other modern languages, there exist no manuscripts of so ancient date containing fairy tales. In view of this fact, the method adopted in this chapter is to develop the idea of the typical Celtic fairy mistress story on the basis of Irish material, using the two or three Welsh tales whose ancient character is perhaps most universally admitted,[3] only as illustrative of incidents the presence

---

[1] Zimmer, *Kuhn's Zt.*, XXVIII, 417 (1887). Cf. Henderson, *Fled Bricrend*, pp. xxiv ff.

[2] Windisch, *Irische Texte*, I, 60.

[3] The Welsh tales used are: *Pwyll Prince of Dyvet* (from the *Red Book of Hergest*) and *The Victims of Annwn*. The Red Book is a fourteenth-century MS.,

of which in Celtic story before the time of Chrétien has been established by the Irish narratives. Thus the validity of the method cannot be impugned on the score of dates. It can only be attacked, therefore, by questioning the closeness of the resemblances between the *Ivain* and Irish story, — a matter which is perfectly open and definite, so that every reader may decide for himself.

It ought, moreover, to be observed that there is *a priori* no reason to insist that, if the Celtic origin of the Iwain story be admitted, the resemblances between it and Irish tales must necessarily be very marked. The Brythonic stories were probably only parallel to the Goidelic, not identical with them, and it is only through the lost Brythonic stories that Celtic influences could have reached Chrétien. Irish tales are therefore two removes from Chrétien. The fact, then, that we do find marked resemblances between them and the *Ivain* must under the circumstances be regarded as doubly significant.

Apparently the most primitive in form of Celtic fairy mistress stories is that describing the adventures of Connla the Fair, which is proved by considerations of language to have been originally written down as early as the ninth century. The manuscript in which the tale is preserved is the *Lebor na h-Uidre.*

ECHTRA CONDLA CHAIM.[1]

Why is he called Art All-alone? Not hard! One day Connla, son of Conn of the Hundred Battles, was at his father's side when he saw a woman

---

but mistakes in spelling and the actual existence of some fragments in a thirteenth-century MS. show that the scribe was copying an older text. Loth (*Les Mabinogion*, I, 18) thinks the tales of the Red Book were written down toward the end of the twelfth century. *Pwyll Prince of Dyvet*, however, is one of the four genuine Mabinogion concerning which Loth says (p. 9): "Elles appartiennent au cycle gallois le plus ancien et sont sans doute un reste du patrimoine commun aux Gaëls et aux Bretons." Elsewhere (p. 20) he says: "Elles plongent dans le plus lointain passé de l'histoire des Celtes." *The Victims of Annwn* is put by Stephens (*Lit. of the Kymry*, 2d ed., p. 273) in the twelfth or thirteenth century, but it shows no signs of the influence of French romance. It is preserved in a manuscript dating from the early part of the fourteenth century.

[1] Summarized from the Irish text as printed by Windisch, *Kurzgefasste Irische Grammatik*, pp. 118–120. For a French translation, see d'Arbois de Jubainville,

in wonderful garments coming to him.   She invited him to the Fields of
the Living, to enjoy "perpetual feasts without preparation, where king
Boadag is an everlasting king without complaint and without grief in his
land since he took the kingdom."   The land is one of peace, and the
people are the peaceful people.[1]   The woman declared that she was young,
beautiful, of noble race, not subject to age or decay.   She loved Connla
and had come to invite him to Mag Mell.   She was invisible to every one
but Connla, so that at first Conn wondered to whom his son was speaking.
When he grasped the situation, he had his druid called to drive away the
fairy by the use of spells.

Before the woman departed she gave Connla an apple.   On this apple
he lived for a month, for it was not diminished, however much he ate of
it, but continued entirely untouched.   No other food seemed to him worthy
to be eaten except his apple.   He was, moreover, seized with longing for
the woman that he had seen.

At the end of a month the woman appeared again to Connla.   She spoke
to him of the delights of her land, where death was unknown, and invited
him to enter her boat:

> We must embark in my ship of glass
> If we are to reach Sid Boadaig.
> There is another land, —
> It were not worse for thee to visit it.
> I see the bright sun is setting.
> However far it is, we shall arrive before night.
> It is a land where is joy
> Passing the thought of everyone who visits it (?).
> There is no one dwelling there
> Except women and maidens.

Unable to resist his longing for the woman, Connla made a spring into
her ship of glass, which thereupon withdrew gradually across the sea.   He
has not been seen since that time, nor is it known whither he went.

Art, thus deserted by his brother Connla, returned alone to the assembly.

L'Épopée Celtique, I, 385–390, and F. Lot, *Romania*, XXVII, 559 ff.   For one in
German, see Zimmer, *Zt. f. deutsches Alt.*, XXXIII, 262 ff.   See Nutt, *Voyage of
Bran*, I, 144 ff.

[1] "Æs síde."   This may mean rather "Her land is the land of the *Síd* [fairy
hill] and her people the people of the *Síd*."   Probably the words in the text are
an attempt to etymologize *æs síde*.

When his father saw him approaching thus unaccompanied, he exclaimed : " Art is All-alone to-day ; probably so is not his brother." So from this time the name " All-alone" [*Óenfer*] clung to Art.

Like most Irish fairy tales, this story evidently owes its preservation, not to its intrinsic charm, which surely for a modern reader is very great, but to the purely accidental fact that it has been at some time altered to explain, in a popular way, the name of one of Conn's sons, Art Óenfer. Fortunately the alterations in this case appear to have been very slight, — a mere tag at the beginning and the end, so that there is reason to hold that we have here a Celtic folk tale in practically its primitive form.[1] The story well illustrates the exalted character of the primitive Celtic *fée.* She is really a queen of the Other World. She wooes the mortal hero with an almost haughty condescension. There is no thought of his capturing or outwitting her, as is regularly the case in Germanic fairy tales. She seeks out the hero and lures him away to her own land, from which he never returns.

The story is really an Other-World Journey. The *fée* lives across the sea, so that we have a hint of what is technically known as the *imram.*[2] The landscape of the Other World is not described. We learn, however, that it is a land of perpetual youth, where, without the intervention of a throng of servants, a never-ending feast is always ready. It is a land inhabited by women only. It possesses magic food that fails not, and is reached in a magic boat that accomplishes any distance before night. The *fée* herself has the power of being invisible to every one except him whom she seeks. All these traits reappear continually in later tales. Their occurrence in this very ancient story is evidence of the substantial continuity of Irish tradition.

---

[1] Probably the number of tales of this sort current in Ireland from pagan times on was very considerable, as indeed it continues to be down to the present day. Only a few of these, either because they were connected with some historical personage, or because they were made to explain some proper name, had the good fortune to be written down and preserved in MS.

[2] I distinguish between the genuine *imram*, a literary product, where stress is laid on the incidents of a voyage by sea and on the different islands visited, and the simple Other-World Journey, where, as here, though a voyage is mentioned, no importance is attached to it.

Another very ancient tale, which has, however, suffered complete remodelling by euhemeristic hands, is that called *The Debility of the Ultonian Warriors*. This is one of the *remscéla* ("introductory tales") brought into close connection with the famous *Táin Bó Cúailgne*. An original fairy mistress story has been altered to explain in a popular manner the extraordinary debility that befell the Ultonian warriors in the *Táin Bó* at the moment when they were attacked by the forces of Medb.[1]

NOINDEN ULAD.[2]

Whence comes the Debility of the Ultonians? Not hard! Crunniuc, son of Agnoman, was a wealthy farmer. One day, as he was alone in his house, a woman of stately appearance entered. She seated herself and began to prepare food as if she had been in the house before. [She passed a whole day there without exchanging a word with any one.][3] When it was night, she gave directions to the servants without a question. She slept beside Crunniuc that night and remained with him for a long time.

One day there was an assembly held by the Ultonians to which they were accustomed to go, both men and women, sons and daughters. Crunniuc made ready to go with the others. ["Go not, said his wife, lest you run into danger by speaking of us; *for our union will continue* only if you do not speak of me in the assembly."][4] "That shall not be," said he.

---

[1] This debility, which lasted for five nights and four days, whence the name *Noinden*, was perhaps really a sort of *couvade:* see Rhŷs, *Hibbert Lectures*, pp. 140, 363, and, for references on this strange custom, Suchier, *Aucassin und Nicolete*, 4th ed., pp. 54–55; Tylor, *Researches into the Early History of Mankind*, pp. 289–297. Miss Hull, however, suggests that it originated rather in a sort of *tabu* (*Cuchullin Saga*, p. 293).

[2] Summarized from the Irish text in the *Book of Leinster* as printed by Windisch, *Berichte der Gesellschaft der Wissenschaften zu Leipzig*, Phil.-hist. Classe, XXXVI, 336 ff. (1884). The story is found also in the later MSS. *Harleian 5280* (about 1560), *The Book of Fermoy* (fifteenth century), *The Yellow Book of Lecan* (fourteenth century). The Harleian text with a translation was printed by Windisch (l.c.). For a French translation, see d'Arbois, *L'Épopée Celtique*, I, 320 ff.; cf. E. Hull, *Cuchullin Saga*, pp. 77–100.

[3] This sentence is not in LL. I insert it from the Harleian text.

[4] This sentence is from the Harleian MS. In place of it LL. reads: "'It befits you,' said his wife, 'not to be overconfident and speak recklessly.'"

The assembly was held. Toward the end of the day the king's chariot with its horses won the victory. The people cried : " There is nothing swifter than these horses ! " But Crunniuc said : " My wife is swifter." He was instantly seized by the king and ordered to be put to death unless he could prove his rash words. A messenger was sent to tell his wife. " It is truly a misfortune for me," said she, " that I must go to free him, for I am with child." The woman, however, went to the assembly and ran the race to save her husband. She reached the goal before the horses, but was delivered of twins on the spot and died. In her agony she screamed, and all the men who heard her cry fell into a weakness like that of a woman in travail for five nights and four days. This weakness returned periodically till the ninth generation : hence the *Noinden Ulad*. The woman's name was Macha, daughter of Sainreth mac Imbaith.

In the above outline I have at two points (marked by brackets) followed the Harleian manuscript rather than the *Book of Leinster*, because at these points the later manuscript seems to me to have suffered less from the hands of the euhemerizer. In any case, the original fairy character of the lady appears beyond dispute. Her ancestry as given in the *Book of Leinster* is enough to indicate this : " Macha, daughter of Sainreth ('strange'), son of Imbath (ocean)." [1] That is to say : daughter of the Stranger and granddaughter of the Sea. She is therefore of the race of Manannán son of Ocean, who, as we shall see, plays an important part in most Celtic fairy tales.[2]

This story is important because its great antiquity is supported, not only by the external evidence already set forth, but by the primitive savagery attributed in it to the king, a bit of internal testimony sufficiently significant of itself. Taken together, these two stories, the *Connla* and the *Noinden*, whose ancient character is assured, seem to show that of the different conceptions of the *fée*, that which regarded her as a supreme being to whom every one else in the Other World is subject, was the older. In the *Connla*, to be sure, a king (Boadag) of Mag Mell is mentioned, but, as nothing is told about

---

[1] D'Arbois de Jubainville has pointed this out (*L'Épopée Celtique*, I, 325). The meaning of *imbath* (= ocean) is supported by Cormac's *Glossary*, p. 94.

[2] Manannán mac Lir, who appears in the Welsh tales of the *Red Book of Hergest* as Manawyddan ab Llyr, an Other-World power.

him and as the land is said to be inhabited by women only, perhaps he is a mere name inserted because it was felt that every land must have a king. Certainly it does not appear that he had power to limit in any way the liberty of the *fée*. In the euhemerized *Noinden* the most distinguishing feature of the original story, so far as we can make out, must have been that in it the position of the *fée* was so exalted that a single disobedience to her directions brought as its punishment[1] perpetual separation.

In the Irish tales next to be taken up (which are perhaps of later origin or at least are not preserved in so primitive forms as the

---

[1] A parallel to the *Noinden* may be found in the Latin of Walter Map, *De Nugis Curialium*, ii, 12. The tale is told of Wild Edric, who was lord of Ledbury North, a place in Hereford on the borders of Wales, and therefore very likely goes back to Welsh tradition. If so, it has suffered modification under Teutonic influence, for it represents the hero as carrying off the fairy, an incident never found in genuine ancient Celtic story. The true Celtic *fée* is never surprised. She is far too exalted for that. She always comes of herself, as in the *Noinden*, — an important distinction between it and the tale of Edric. In other respects, however, the story is so much like that of the *Noinden* (in both the *fée* is silent at first for a long time; in both she disappears when the prohibition is broken) that it may rest at bottom on a Welsh fairy mistress tale. If so, it is an example of the substantial parallelism of Welsh and Irish tradition. "One day as Edricus Wilde was returning from the hunt, accompanied only by a lad, he lost his way in the forest. About midnight he came to a brilliantly lighted house (*ghildhus*), within which he saw a band of noble women engaged in a solemn dance. One, more beautiful than the rest, charmed him beyond measure. Fired with love, he rushed into the house and forcibly carried off the object of his passion. She *remained mute for three days, though she did not refuse his caresses.* On the fourth day she spoke, saying : 'Hail, my dearest! *You will be happy and prosperous till the day that you reproach me* concerning the place or the wood in which I was found or concerning anything of the sort.' Edric promised to be faithful in his love. But some years later he chanced to return from the hunt at the third hour of the night. He called for his wife, and when she was long in appearing, he cried angrily : 'Pray, is it your sisters that have so long detained you?' At the words she instantly vanished. Edric mourned exceedingly, and visited again the place whence he had carried her off, but he was unable to call her back by any entreaties. He wept day and night even to the point of foolishness toward himself, for he wore out his life in perpetual grief." Cf. also Liebrecht, *Die Todten von Lustnau, Germania*, XIII, 161 ff. (and *Zur Volkskunde*, pp. 54 ff.), where many similar tales are cited.

Connla and the *Noinden*), although the *fée* retains the exalted position which is a distinctive mark of Celtic tradition, she is no longer absolutely independent. There are kings as well as queens of the Other World. The *fée* is regarded as the wife or the daughter of the king of Mag Mell. With the intrusion of the masculine element has come also the idea of combat. The Other World is no longer altogether a Land of Peace.

It is easy to see how these ideas may have been developed from the notion of a king of the Other World found already in the *Connla*. It is possible also that they may have existed from the earliest times side by side with the conception of the *fée* as supreme in authority over a land of peace. But the fact that the latter view is indicated in the two oldest tales is at least significant.

More important, however, is the consideration that in the *Serglige Conculaind* (the most complete of all the ancient tales of this *genre*), in which the *fée* is represented as the wife of Manannán, and in which a combat in the Other World is an important feature, all the leading parts are played by women. It is a fairy woman, Liban, who comes as a messenger to Cuchulinn and conducts him through the dangerous passage, and a woman, the *fée* herself, comes part way to meet him. The other-world actors in the story are all women. It looks, therefore, as if the men were originally mere servants or dependents of the *fée*.

Although the story of *Cuchulinn's Sick Bed* is tolerably accessible, yet, on account of its importance to this investigation, I have ventured to outline it at considerable length, following the Irish text as edited by Windisch.[1]

SERGLIGE CONCULAIND.

Two birds linked together by a chain of gold visited a lake in Ulster and by their song put the host to sleep. Cuchulinn, though warned that

---

[1] *Irische Texte*, I, 197–227, from the *Lebor na h-Uidre*, where it is said to be extracted from "The Yellow Book of Slane," evidently an earlier MS. For English translations of the tale, see O'Curry, *Atlantis*, I, 362–392, II, 98–124 (1858); O'Looney in J. T. Gilbert, *Facsimiles of National MSS.*, I, 27–28, II, App. iv (1874–78). For a French translation, see d'Arbois de Jubainville, *L'Épopée Celtique*, I, 170–216. Cf. Zimmer, *Kuhn's Zt.*, XXVIII, 594 ff.

there was "some power behind the birds," sought to slay them (§ 7).[1]
Being unsuccessful, he went away in bad spirits, and, sitting down against
an upright stone, fell asleep.   He saw two women come towards him, one
in green and one in a five-folded crimson cloak.   The woman in green went
up to him and laughed and gave him a stroke of a whip.   Then the other,
coming up, also laughed and struck him, and this they did alternately till
they left him nearly dead (§ 8).[2]

He was carried into a house, where he lay till the end of a year without
speaking to any one (§ 9).   Then, as he lay in the bed, a man mysteriously
appeared, who sang verses promising him health and strength if he would
accept the invitation of the daughters of Aed Abrat, one of whom, named
Fand, wished to marry Cuchulinn (§ 10).   The man departed after that,
and they knew not whence he came or whither he went (§ 12).   Cuchulinn
rose up and spoke and went back to the upright stone, where he saw again
the woman in the green cloak.   From her he learned that Fand, deserted
by her husband Manannán mac Lir, had fallen in love with him.   Her
own name is Liban.   She is sister to Fand and wife to Labraid Swift-
Hand-on-Sword, who has sent her to ask Cuchulinn for one day's assistance
against Labraid's enemies, Senach Síabortha, Eochaid Iúil, and Eogan
Inbir, promising in return to give him Fand to wife.

Cuchulinn sent his charioteer Loeg to see the mysterious land from which
she came (§ 13).   Liban and he went till they came to the place where
Fand was waiting for them.   Then, it is said, Liban took hold of Loeg by
the shoulder.   " O Loeg," said Fand, " thou wilt not come out alive to-day
unless a woman protect thee !"   " I have not been much accustomed to
woman's protection," was Loeg's reply.   Then they came to the water's
edge, where they entered a boat of bronze and crossed over to an island
(§ 14).   Loeg saw Labraid and his palace and returning told his story to
Cuchulinn and to every one else (§§ 16, 20).

Again [3] Liban came to invite Cuchulinn to Mag Mell.   She sang:

> Labraid is over a pure lake
> In a place that bands of women frequent.

---

[1] The references are to Windisch's sections.

[2] Cf. *Perlesvaus*, Potvin, I, 7, where a squire, wounded in a dream, wakes and
finds the knife in his side.

[3] Zimmer, *Kuhn's Zt.*, XXVIII, 600, in his demonstration of the compilatory
character of the sagas in LU, well says that this double preliminary visit of Loeg,
as well as the double invitation by Liban, must have arisen from the contamination
of two different versions of Cuchulinn's adventures.

> It would not be tedious to thee to go to his people
> If thou art to visit Labraid Luath.
>
> . . . . .
>
> A bridle of gold is on his horses,
> And it is not only this,
> A pillar of silver and of glass, —
> This it is which is in his house (§ 31).

"I will not go," said Cuchulinn, "at a woman's invitation." "Let Loeg come then," replied Liban, "to know everything." "Let him go," said Cuchulinn. Loeg therefore went with Liban and came to the place where Fand and Labraid were. Fand said: "Let Cuchulinn come with speed, for it is to-day that the battle is appointed" (§ 32). Thus admonished, Loeg returned, in company with Fand, to Cuchulinn, and sang these verses in praise of the land he had seen:

> I came in the fraction of a moment
> To a place wonderful although known,
> Up to a cairn with a band of twenty,
> Where I found Labraid Long-Hair.
>
> . . . . .
>
> There were two kings in the house,
> Failbe Find and Labraid.
> Three fifties about each of them,
> This was the number of one house.
> Fifty beds on the right side
> And fifty their burden (?),
> Fifty beds on the left side
> And fifty their burden (?).
> Front rails to the beds of wood,
> Their posts of white gilded over,
> And the light that they have
> Is a precious glittering stone.
> There is at the door toward the west,
> In the place where the sun goes down,
> A stud of pale horses with gay manes;
> There is another, purple brown;
> There are at the door toward the east
> Three trees of shining purple
> From which calls down the flock of birds,
> Always gentle to the youths from the royal city.
> There is a tree at the door of the enclosure,
> Not hateful the harmony from it,
> A tree of silver; against it the sun shines,

Like unto gold its great splendor.
There are three-score trees,
Their tops barely touching.
Three hundred men are nourished by each tree,
With fruit manifold, without rind.
There is a well in the noble *síd*,
With three fifties, gay mantled;
And a brooch of gold, fair its color,
In every one of the gay mantles.
There is a cask there with joyous mead,
Which is distributed to the household.
It continues ever, enduring is the custom,
So that it is always constantly full.
There is a woman in this noble house;
She is superior to the women of Ireland;
With golden hair she comes out
In her accomplished beauty.
Her speech to the men of each king
Is beautiful, is wonderful.
She breaks the heart of every man
For her love and her affection.

Loeg declared that so great was her beauty as to cause him "to fear for his honor." He added :

If there were to me all Ireland
And the kingdom with the yellow hills,
I would give it — no slight temptation —
For the company in the place to which I came (§ 33).
If I had not come away quickly,
They had wounded me so that I had been powerless.

. . . .

The woman whom I speak of there,
She robs the hosts of their wits (§ 34).

Cuchulinn, persuaded by these words, mounted his chariot and accompanied Loeg and Fand to Mag Mell (§ 35). The combat now took place. At early dawn, Cuchulinn transfixed with his spear Eochaid Iúil, who was washing himself at a well. After that, he slew Senach Síabortha and won a victory for Labraid (§ 36). In return, he received Fand, with whom he lived for a month. When he departed she said to him : "I will meet thee in whatever place thou shalt appoint for me to come."

After Cuchulinn returned home, he revealed to his wife Emer the appointed place of meeting. The jealous queen lay in wait with knives to murder Fand. Cuchulinn rescued her (§ 39), but when Manannán mac Lir heard of it, he suddenly appeared, visible to Fand alone. When she saw him she sang :

> See the son of the host of Lir
> Across the plains of Eógan Inbir!
> It is Manannán more beautiful than the world.
> There was a time when he was dear to me.
>
> . . . .
>
> I see over the ocean yonder —
> No foolish person sees him —
> The Horseman of the Hairy Sea.
> He is not accompanied by a boat.
> In his approach he has passed by us here.
> No one sees him except fairy folk (§ 45).

Thereupon Fand forsook Cuchulinn and went with Manannán (§ 46). When Cuchulinn perceived his loss of Fand, " he sprang three leaps upward and three leaps to the right of Lúacra, so that he was for a long time without drink and without food among the mountains, and 't is there that he slept every night upon the road of Midlúacra " (§ 47).

Emer persuaded Conchobar to send "poets and people of wisdom and druids of the Ulstermen " to heal Cuchulinn, but " he sought to murder the people of wisdom. However, they sang their druidical charms over him till they captured his feet and hands and till he recovered a little of his senses. He asked for a drink then. They gave him a drink of forgetfulness." As he drank the drink, there was no recollection to him of Fand nor of anything that he had done. Manannán shook his cloak between Cuchulinn and Fand so that they should never meet again (§ 48).

This is the oldest known example of that particular type of Celtic fairy mistress story to which, on the hypothesis of a Celtic source, the original tale of Iwain must have belonged. The story, it will be observed, shows no noticeable modification by either Christian or classical influences. It appears, therefore, to embody genuine pagan tradition,[1] though, as I have hinted, it may not be so old a form of the type as that which represents the *fée* as altogether supreme. The

---

[1] Whether the primitive Celtic character of the story be admitted or not, is, however, of no consequence to the question of Chrétien's source. For the purposes of this study, it is enough to know that the story in its present form was current among the Celts at the time when LU was written.

tale of course owes its preservation to the fact that it is told of the great hero Cuchulinn, who was regarded as an historical personage.[1] In the same way, the original tale of Iwain, from which, according to the hypothesis, Chrétien drew, was connected no doubt with the historical Owen, a hero of the Brythonic Celts.

The resemblances between the story of Cuchulinn's Other-World Journey and the *Ivain* may be put somewhat compactly as follows : In the *Serglige*, it is the account given by a previous adventurer, Loeg, that stirs Cuchulinn to undertake the Other-World Journey. The same is true in the *Ivain*, where the tale of Calogrenant supplies the incentive. In both stories the encounter with the Other-World folk is provoked by going to a particular spot and performing a particular act. Cuchulinn sits down against an upright stone ; Iwain pours water on the stone at the Fountain Perilous. The Other-World landscape as described by Loeg reminds one distinctly of the marvellous scenery at the Fountain Perilous. In both there is a tree from which a flock of birds sings with harmony, while close at hand is "a noble well." Loeg's description of the beauty of Fand, "which robs the hosts of their wits," reads like an extract from Iwain's reflections at the sight of Laudine. There is a dangerous passage on the way to the Other World, according to the *Serglige*, from which Loeg is told that he will not return alive unless a woman protects him. Liban therefore takes him by the shoulder at this point. Similarly in the *Ivain* the hero escapes from the peril at the falling gates by the aid of a woman, Lunete, who is, like Liban, the messenger and *confidante* of the lady.[2] In both stories the hero must be

---

[1] The best authorities still so regard him (see Zimmer, *Keltische Studien*, II, 189).

[2] Chrétien does not say that Lunete is, like Liban, the sister of the lady, but he represents her as occupying such a position of influence that it is natural to think that she may have been, in a more primitive form of the tale, the lady's sister. Cf. *Ivain*, vv. 1589 ff. :

> La dameisele estoit si bien
> De sa dame que nule rien
> A dire ne li redotast,
> A quoi que la chose tornast,
> Qu'ele estoit sa mestre et sa garde.

In *Le Bel Inconnu* the messenger is a sister of the enchanted lady for whom she seeks help at Arthur's court, and so in other similar stories.

the victor in a combat before he secures the lady's hand.   Cuchulinn slays Eochaid Iúil and Senach Síabortha.   Iwain slays Esclados the Red.   In both, the hero marries the lady.   In both, he leaves her to return to his own land.   In both, for a slight offense (in the *Serglige*, because of his having revealed to his wife the appointed place of meeting; in the *Ivain* for having overstayed his time), he loses her.   In both, the result is the madness of the hero, who runs wild in the forests or on the mountains.[1]   In both cases he is cured by a marvellous remedy : Iwain by an ointment of "Morgue la sage," Cuchulinn by a druidical " drink of forgetfulness."   In carrying this parallel out, Laudine naturally equates with Fand,[2] Lunete with Liban,

---

[1] Cuchulinn, it is said, " went without drink and without food."   Iwain's hunger in the same situation is thus described in v. 2852 : " Mes li fains l'angoisse et esforce."

[2] The meaning of the name Fand is given in the *Serglige* ("Fand ainm na dére " : Windisch, *Irische Texte*, I, 210) as "tear-drop."   Manannán, son of Ocean, is evidently a sea divinity.   Rhŷs is perhaps therefore right in identifying this Liban, daughter of Aed Abrat, with a Liban, daughter of Eocho, who, in the story called the *Destruction of Eocho mac Mairedo* (in LU, 39, *a* 22 ff., edited and translated by Crowe, *Proceedings of R. H. and A. A. of Ireland*, 187c, pp. 94–112 ; the same tale, from a late MS., is in O'Grady, *Silv. Gad.*, II, 267 ff.), is a woman in charge of a magic well, which, neglected by her, overwhelmed her and changed her into a mermaid, half salmon, half woman (Rhŷs, *Hib. Lect.*, p. 463, mistakenly says into " an otter "), while the water formed Loch Neagh.   After she had ranged the sea for three hundred years, Beon heard her singing beneath his boat.   She told him that she had come on purpose to make an appointment to meet him a year hence.   On that day she was caught.   Comgall baptized her *Muirghein* (sea-birth).

The Land *beyond* the Waves, where the fairy folk are represented as dwelling (cf. Labraid's Isle in the *Serglige*), was no doubt confused with the Land *beneath* the Waves, just as Zimmer has shown that the Fairies of the Síd and the Fairies of the Land beyond the Waves are never kept separate (*Zt. f. deutsches Alt.*, XXXIII, 276).   It is not, therefore, surprising to find the people of the Other World provided with names appropriate to the waters (cf. Macha, granddaughter of the Sea, in the *Noinden*).   That the Celtic Other World was early confused with the Land beneath the Waves is clear from the tale of *Loegaire mac Crimthann* in the *Book of Leinster*.   This story has never been translated from the ancient manuscript.   A translation from a fifteenth century manuscript may be found in O'Grady, *Silva Gadelica*, II, 290–291.   The following outline is made from the R. I. A. *Book of Leinster Facsimile*, 275, β, 22—276, β, 20 :

and Esclados with Manannán, son of Ocean, for Cuchulinn secures the love of Fand after the departure of Manannán, just as Iwain does that of Laudine after the death of Esclados. The *fée* is in both tales already married to a husband, with whom possession of her must be disputed.

Crimthann Cas, king of Connaught, held a great assembly by Bird Lake in the plain of Aei. When the host arose early in the morning, they saw approaching through the mist a man in a five-folded purple mantle. A gold-rimmed shield was slung on him, a gold-hilted sword was in his belt, and golden hair streamed behind him. The stranger was welcomed by Loegaire, the king's son, to whom he declared that he was Fiachna mac Retach of the Fairy Folk. His wife has been

The Tale of
Loegaire. carried off by a hostile prince. He has fought several unsuccessful battles to recover her, and this very day another battle is appointed. It is to solicit help that he is come. "Not to aid this man were a shameful thing," said Loegaire, and together with fifty fighting men he stepped out after the stranger, who, still preceding them, dived into the *loch,* and they followed him [*Gaibidside remib fón loch. Gabaitseom dono ina dhiaid.* 276, *a*, 20]. When they reached Mag Mell, they engaged in the battle against Fiachna's enemy Goll. Goll was slain, and Fiachna's wife was rescued. That night Fiachna's daughter was bestowed on Loegaire, and on his fifty lads fifty other women. So to a year's end they abode.

One day Loegaire asked leave to go and seek tidings of his land. "If ye would come back," Fiachna enjoined, "take horses with you and by no means dismount from them." So when he and his companions had reached their own land of Connaught, their friends rushed forth to meet them, but were warned off by Loegaire, who said, "Touch us not; 'tis to bid you farewell that we are here." "Leave me not!" implored his father Crimthann. But Loegaire sang: "One night of the nights of the Síd I would not give for thy kingdom." So he turned from them and entered the Síd, where with Fiachna he exercised kingly rule and the daughter of Fiachna beside him.

A striking parallel to this prohibition of dismounting is to be found in what we must regard as essentially the Welsh tale of Herla (Walter Map, *De Nugis*, It 11), "a king of the very ancient Britons," who visited the Under World and on returning was given a dog and warned not to allow any of his train to dismount till the dog had done so. Herla, on coming out into daylight, found that he had been absent more than two hundred years, though it seemed but three days. One of his train dismounted, disregarding the injunction respecting the dog, and forthwith fell in a heap of dust. As the dog has not yet dismounted, Herla and his train are compelled to wander over the world. On the punishment for dismounting, cf. the fate of Nechtan, *Voyage of Bran*, § 65, and that of Guingamor (see Schofield, in *Studies and Notes*, V, 221 ff.). Other parallels might easily be collected.

The diligent reader of Arthurian material must feel a certain probability in this parallel between Esclados le Ros and Manannán, the tricky magician and shape-shifter of the Celts.[1] The mysterious

---

[1] Rhŷs, *Hib. Lect.*, pp. 370–371, suggests a connection between Manannán and the Irish stem *mon-* (" a trick "). The shape-shifting character of Manannán is well established. In a quotation from the *Tain Bó* (LU) in O'Curry's *Manners and Customs*, II, 310, it is said: "Cuchulinn threw his mantle of invisibility over him, manufactured from the precious fleeces of the land of the immortals, which had been brought him by Manannán mac Lir." In the *Book of Leinster*, 152, β, 16, we read that one of Manannán's messengers, Fer-Fí, had the power of assuming at pleasure a woman's shape. In some fragmentary Annals in *Egerton 1782*, a fifteenth century MS. (translated by O'Grady, *Silva Gad.*, II, 425), it is said : "The notable Mongan was son to that same Fiachna ; for albeit certain dealers in antiquarian fables do propound him to have been son to Manannán, and wont to enter at his pleasure into diverse shapes, yet this we may not credit," where the connection felt between Manannán and shape-shifting is clear. In the *Legend of Eithne*, in the *Book of Fermoy*, a fifteenth century MS. (summarized by Todd, *R. I. A., Irish MS. Series*, I, i, 46), we are told that Manannán was the great astrologer and magician of the Tuatha De Danaan. He settled them in the most beautiful valleys, drawing round them an invisible wall, impenetrable to the eyes of other men, and impassable. Manannán also supplied them with the ale of Goibhnenn the Smith, which preserved them from old age and death, and gave them for food his own swine, which, although killed and eaten one day, were alive again and fit for eating the next, and so would continue for ever. In the *Sons of Usnech*, edited and translated in *Irische Texte*, II, ii, 109–184, Naisi exclaims (p. 171): "Behold the sword of Manannán mac Lir. It leaves no relic of stroke or blow behind." In the *Fate of the Children of Tuirenn* (translated by Joyce, *Old Celtic Romances*, pp. 36 ff., from a fifteenth century MS.) Luge is described as possessing a full set of Manannán's belongings : "He rode Manannán's steed *Enbarr* of the flowing mane. No one was ever killed on this steed, for she travelled with equal ease on land and on sea. He wore Manannán's coat of mail, through which no one could be wounded. He had on Manannán's breast plate, that no weapon could pierce, and Manannán's helmet *Cannbarr*, that glittered with dazzling brightness (p. 49). Manannán's sword, *The Answerer*, hung at his side ; no one ever recovered from its wound. Those who were opposed to it in battle had no more strength in looking at it than a woman in violent sickness." (There is a remarkable parallel in this sword to Caliburnus, Geoffrey, ix, 4.) Manannán is connected with the Isle of Man, which was perhaps confused by the early Celts with the Land beyond the Waves. There is in Cormac's *Glossary* and in the *Yellow Book of Lecan* (Skene, *Four Books*, I, 79; Rhŷs, *Hib. Lect.*, p. 664) a strictly euhemerized account of him, which yet lays stress on his shrewdness : "Manannán mac Lir, a celebrated merchant between Erin, Alban and the Isle of Man. A druid

red knight[1] who encountered Iwain at the fountain has absolutely no character of his own. One cannot but fancy that he was, in an earlier form of the story, some one in disguise.

It is convenient for the purpose of illustration to arrange the incidents of the *Serglige* and those of the *Ivain* in parallel columns, as on the following page.

From this table it will be seen that of the seventeen incidents which make up the main portion of the *Ivain*,[2] ten may be traced

---

(i.e. magician) was he also, and he was the best navigator, and used to know through his science the calms and storms." Modern Celtic folk-tales agree in representing Manannán as a shape-shifter (cf. Larminie, *West Irish Folk-Tales*, p. 64, and especially *Gloss Gavlen*, Larminie, pp. 1–9).

It is plain, from a poem in the *Black Book of Caermarthen* (written before 1189) that this character of Manannán was shared by the ancient Welsh Manawyddan ab Llyr. See Skene, *Four Books*, I, 262 (text, II, 51) :

> Manawydan the son of Llyr,
> Deep was his counsel.
> Did not Manawyd bring
> Perforated shields from Trywruid ?

In the *Book of Taliesin* (fourteenth century MS.), Skene, I, 276 (text II, 153), he is connected with the Other World :

> Complete is my chair in Caer Sidi . . .
> It is known to Manawyd and Pryderi.

In the Mabinogi of *Manawyddan ab Llyr* (Loth, *Les Mabinogion*, I, 97 ff.) he is represented as outwitting Llwyd ab Kilcoet, the greatest enchanter of Britain. Perhaps the numerous different trades that Manawyddan successively takes up in this tale are a relic of his habit of assuming different shapes.

[1] See pp. 114 ff., below.

[2] The *Serglige* furnishes no parallel to the latter portion of the *Ivain*. Celtic fairy mistress tales usually end, as the *Ivain* appears to do, with a reconciliation between the hero and the *fée*, and his permanent residence with her in the Other World. Whether the original tale of Fand ended in this way or not, such a *dénouement* could not be retained when the story was worked up into its present form as a definite part of the Cuchulinn saga, for the later adventures and the death of Cuchulinn are there related. We may suppose, therefore, that the original ending of the *Serglige* has suffered modification. The first part of the *Serglige* is not paralleled in the *Ivain*. It is to be noted, however, in regard to the coming of Liban to invite Cuchulinn to the Other World (incident 4 of the table), that Lunete is made to say in the *Ivain* (vv. 1004 ff.) that she had been sent once as

SERGLIGE CONCULAIND.	CHRÉTIEN'S IVAIN.	MATRON OF EPHESUS.
1. Visit of Mysterious Birds	1. *Calogrenant's Previous Visit.*	1. —
2. Sickness of the Hero	2. Hospitable Host.	2. —
3. An Other-World Visitor	3. Giant Herdsman.	3. —
4. Meeting with Lady's Confidante	4. *Marvellous Landscape.*	4. —
5. Loeg's Visit to the Other World	5. Rain-Making Fountain.	5. —
6. A Perilous Passage	6. *Combat with Esclados.*	6. —
7. Protection by Lady's Confidante	7. Falling Gates.	7. —
8. Other-World Landscape	8. *Protection by Lady's Confidante.*	8. A kindly Confidante.
9. Effects of Fand's Beauty	9. Invisible-Rendering Ring.	9. —
10. Combat in the Other World	10. Warrior is the Lady's Husband.	10. —
11. Marriage with Fand	11. Corpse bleeds before the Slayer.	11. —
12. Departure of Cuchulinn	12. *Effects of the Lady's Beauty.*	12. —
13. Broken Faith and Madness	13. *Marriage with the Lady.*	13. Remarriage of newly bereaved Widow.
14. Cure by Magic Remedy	14. Arrival of King Arthur.	14. —
	15. *Departure of the Hero.*	15. —
	16. Broken Promise and Madness.	16. —
[Not parallelled in the *Serglige.*]	17. *Cure by Magic Remedy.*	17. —
	18. Helpful Lion.	18. —
	19. Conflicting Appointments.	19. —
	20. Combat with Giant Harpin.	20. —
	21. Rescue of Damsel by Judicial Combat.	21. —
	22. Daughters of the Black Thorn.	22. —
	23. Castle of Ill Adventure.	23. —
	24. Combat of Fratres Jurati.	24. —
	25. Reconciliation of Herc and Lady.	25. —

more or less distinctly in the older tale. The arrangement of the episodes, too, is essentially the same, for incidents 6 and 7 of the *Serglige* have been inserted in the table from Loeg's narrative. It would be fair to transpose them to the later journey of Cuchulinn, of which of course they must have been episodes also.

The table is given at this point as an aid to the study of the Other-World Journey type of story. It is not maintained that by itself it proves much. Doubtless one or two of the parallels noted, as perhaps that between the perilous passage encountered by Loeg and the falling gates in the *Ivain*, may for the present seem not to be significant. But the matter does not end here. We are able, and this will be our next task, to trace these motives through the mass of Celtic Other-World story and thus determine their typical development. In this way it will be possible to ascertain what the significance of the parallels here indicated really is. The table serves to make it plain that parallels of some sort to most of the incidents of the main portion of the *Ivain* can be pointed out in this one ancient story, which, it must be remembered, is, so to speak, two removes from Chrétien. In the first place, it is a Goidelic and not a Brythonic tale, and, in the second place, Chrétien either did not understand the Other-World character of what, according to the hypothesis, we must suppose to have been the essentially Brythonic material he was using, or else he deliberately rationalized it so far as he was able.

For the present, it is plain that enough striking resemblances have been observed to make the theory that the *Ivain* is at bottom an Other-World tale parallel to the *Serglige*, at least very plausible. If we take but four significant parallels, — (1) the fact that both Cuchulinn and Iwain are persuaded to their journey by the tale of a previous adventurer; (2) Loeg's description of the Other-World landscape, which is very like that at the Fountain Perilous; (3) the parallel between Liban, the messenger and *confidante* of Fand, and Lunete ; (4) the madness of the hero consequent upon the loss of the mistress in both stories, — surely we have here at least a better framework,

---

a messenger by her lady to Arthur's court. Perhaps, therefore, an older form of the tale of Iwain had a parallel here. Lunete may have been sent to Arthur's court to invite one of his knights to the marvellous land where her lady dwelt.

out of which we may suppose that Chrétien built up his romance, than the *Matron of Ephesus* could ever furnish. In the *Matron of Ephesus* one can find at most but two motives parallel to the *Ivain*, — the remarriage of a newly bereaved widow, and the presence of a lady's maid or *confidante* who favors the suitor. Whatever discretion, therefore, at this point the reader may exercise about drawing too definite conclusions as to the certainty of a Celtic origin for the *Ivain*, the *Matron of Ephesus* hypothesis must, it would seem, from now on, be regarded as permanently disposed of.

CHAPTER IV (*Continued*).

ANCIENT CELTIC STORIES OF THE JOURNEY TO THE OTHER WORLD.

II. THE COMBAT MOTIVE.

FROM the *Serglige*, as well as from the *Tale of Loegaire* (where as a reward for his aid the hero receives the daughter of the fairy king), it is clear that participation in a successful combat in the Other World was very early [1] represented as a necessary condition for winning the hand of a *fée*. In these two stories, however, the parallel to the *Ivain* is not very close, because it is a general battle, not a single combat like that with Esclados, which is described. It is interesting, therefore, to compare at this point an ancient Welsh tale in which a distinct account of a single combat in the Other World appears:

PWYLL AND ARAWN.[2]

Arawn, a king of the Other World (*Annwn*), appeared to Pwyll, prince of Dyfed in Wales, and proposed an exchange of kingdoms, his object

---

[1] Though, as has been hinted, perhaps not in the earliest tales.

[2] Summarized from *Pwyll Prince of Dyvet*, one of the four genuine Mabinogion. See Loth, *Les Mabinogion*, I, 27–38, and, for the Welsh text, Rhŷs and Evans, *Red Book*, I, 1–8.

being to have the other take his place in a single combat which had been appointed for a certain day one year from that time.[1]   The antagonist was Hafgan, an Other-World king with whom Arawn was continually at war. Arawn declared to Pwyll : " I will set thee in my place in Annwn and give thee the most beautiful woman thou hast ever seen to sleep with thee every night.   And I will put my shape and semblance on thee, so that not a page of the chamber that has always followed me shall know that it is not I. I will take thy kingdom and will cause that no one in all thy dominions shall know that I am not thou."   Pwyll agreed to this, and went to *Annwn* in Arawn's shape, where he took his place beside a queen of wondrous beauty.[2]   When the day appointed for the combat was at hand, the fairy hosts assembled.   An officer made this announcement : " The battle is between two kings, and between them only.   Each claims the other's land and territory.   Ye are to remain quiet and allow the two to decide the fight."   Pwyll wounded Hafgan mortally.   Afterwards he re-exchanged [3] with Arawn, who " gave to Pwyll his own proper semblance while he him- self took his own."   When Pwyll returned to Dyfed he found that no one had been aware of his absence, and that his kingdom had been better governed than usual that year.

In this tale Arawn takes the place of Manannán as the husband of the *fée.*   It will be observed that, like the latter, he is a shape- shifter.   He has power to exchange his appearance with that of Pwyll. As in the *Serglige,* a contest between the husband and the mortal hero for the possession of the *fée* seems to be hinted at.   Cuchulinn enjoyed the company of Fand, after she had been forsaken by Manannán, and lost her when her husband returned.   So Pwyll was entertained in Annwn during the absence of Arawn.

There is in the same mabinogi another tale in which the element of contest for the possession of the *fée* comes out clearly :

---

[1] Similarly in the *Serglige* (§ 32) and in the *Tale of Loegaire,* the time of the Other-World combat was already *fixed* before the message came to the mortal hero urging him to participate.   This is a good example of the parallelism of Welsh and Irish story.

[2] The Welsh tale, however, with unprimitive scrupolosity, makes him respect the chastity of Arawn's queen.

[3] The second meeting of Pwyll and Arawn occurs at the same particular spot as the first, just as Cuchulinn returned to the same upright stone (*Serglige,* § 13). Another parallel between Welsh and Irish story.

PWYLL AND GWAWL.[1]

Pwyll visited the summit of a mound concerning which the tradition was that whoever sat there would see a prodigy. Pwyll had no sooner seated himself than he saw a lady riding past on a white horse. She was clad in a garment of shining gold. As no one could tell who she was, he despatched one of his followers to pursue her. After a chase on foot, the man returned, saying that he could not overtake her. Pwyll gave him the swiftest horse he had, but the man was even then unsuccessful. " There was some magic about the lady that kept her always the same distance ahead, though she appeared to be riding slowly." The next day Pwyll returned to the mound. Again he saw the lady. Again he despatched a mounted servant, and again pursuit was unsuccessful. The third day Pwyll himself, mounted on a swift steed, pursued the lady. Finding himself unable to gain on her, he exclaimed : " For the sake of the man whom you love, wait for me !" At his cry she stopped and waited for him to come up. Pwyll never saw a lady so beautiful. She told him she came solely for love of him. She is Rhiannon, who is to be married to Gwawl, a suitor whom she detests. She will have no one unless it be Pwyll. At her suggestion, Pwyll promised to come at the end of a year to rescue her for himself.

At the appointed day Pwyll went, and was received by Rhiannon at a feast. But a petitioner came in and sought a boon. Pwyll rashly promised him whatever he should ask. He asked for Rhiannon. It was Gwawl, the hated suitor, who had disguised himself as a petitioner in order to trick Pwyll.[2] Pwyll's princely honor kept him from breaking his word once given, and he handed Rhiannon over to Gwawl. However, she persuaded Gwawl to depart for a year's time, and before sending Pwyll away she gave him a magic bag, and instructed him how to entrap his hated rival.

At the end of a year the two suitors returned to Rhiannon, and Pwyll entrapped Gwawl in the bag. His enemy once in the bag, Pwyll wound his horn. His warriors, who were in ambush without, entered and seized all who attempted to resist. Each warrior as he passed dealt a blow at the bag. At length, to escape the punishment of the bag, Gwawl consented to release Pwyll from his rash promise. Thus Pwyll remained in possession of Rhiannon.

---

[1] Summarized from Loth, *Les Mabinogion*, I, 38–52. For the Welsh text, see Rhŷs and Evans, *Red Book*, I, 8 ff.

[2] No one recognizes Gwawl. It is probable, therefore, that he, like Manannán and Arawn, had the power of shape-shifting.

Several of the motives traced in the previous tales recur distinctly in this. There is ever a particular spot to which one must resort in order to meet the fairy folk. Cuchulinn returned to the upright stone. Pwyll, in the previous tale, made his way to the spot where he first met Arawn. In the present narrative, it is from the top of a particular mound that Pwyll on three successive days descries the approach of the *fée*. So in the *Ivain*, whoever makes his way to the Fountain Perilous and pours water on the rock, will encounter the hostile knight. One of the notes of the Other-World Journey is that the coming of the hero is always expected. He may fancy that he has stumbled upon the *fée* by chance, but as a matter of fact she has chosen him long before and lured him to her. Not always, as in the *Echtra Condla*, and as here, does she come in person to escort him. But when her messenger appears, as Liban did to Cuchulinn, it is none the less surely at her suggestion.[1]

Although in this tale of Pwyll a set combat with the unearthly suitor for possession of the *fée* is lacking, yet in the episode of the bag a situation of the sort is closely approximated. Certainly, from a story of this type the idea of representing the *fée* as guarded by a suitor or a husband, who must be overthrown before she can be approached, might naturally be developed. In the first place, as we have seen, it is likely that the *fée* was supreme. She dwelt in a Land of Women, where, though there may have been a king, he was a mere name and did not interfere with the perfect liberty of the *fée*. But the tendency to make the Other World a counterpart of this earth was strong. In the *Serglige*, the *Loegaire*, and their Welsh analogues, the notion of fighting is present, and the *fée*, except in the *Tale of Loegaire*, has a husband or a suitor like any mortal woman. From this the step to regarding her as more or less in the power of a warrior, who must be overthrown before she can be reached, is a natural one. Originally this opposing warrior was probably only a creature of the *fée*, sent out by her to test the hero's valor. He may have appeared for this purpose in various gigantic shapes. If so,

---

[1] For this reason it is probable that the previous visit of Lunete to Arthur's court, referred to in *Ivain*, vv. 1004 ff., was at bottom for the purpose of persuading Iwain to his marvellous journey.

the tendency for confusion to arise between this situation, and the common incident of a giant who has a charming wife, or a pretty daughter, who gladly yields herself as prize to the hero who can slay the tyrant, would be strong. Even, therefore, if our analogues stopped here, we might safely explain the situation of Laudine with respect to Esclados, as a natural development of the combat-episode found in the *Serglige* and in the Welsh parallels, most probably helped by confusion with the well-known motive of the giant[1] and the lady. There is evidence that Esclados may have been represented as a giant in an earlier form of the tale. Calogrenant's description of him ("[Il] fu sanz dote Plus granz de moi la teste tote," v. 521. 2) and of his lance ("n'estoit mie legiere, Einz iert plus grosse au mien cuidier Que nule lance a chevalier; Qu' einz nule si grosse ne vi," vv. 534–537) is borne out by the description of the corresponding warrior in the analogous episode of "La Joie de la Cort" in the *Erec:* "Qui mout estoit granz a mervoilles" and

> Estoit un pié plus granz
> A tesmoing de totes les janz,
> Que chevaliers que l'an seüst (vv. 5900–5905).

---

[1] Whoever doubts that the popular tale of a giant with a beautiful captive was current among the ancient Celts should read a passage from the *Tochmarc Emere* (LU, 126, a 11–41), translated and discussed by Zimmer in *Haupt's Zt.*, XXXII, 240–241. The whole saga has since been published by K. Meyer in *Zt. f. Celt. Phil.*, III, 229 (from MS. Harl. 5280). Cuchulinn, on his way to Ireland, stops at an island. He finds the daughter of the king about to be given to two giants (*fomóir*) unless a champion can be found. Cuchulinn slays the giants. Many go to the palace of the king and pretend to have done the deed, but the girl recognizes Cuchulinn. The king thereupon offers his daughter to Cuchulinn, who refuses her and departs. The incident of others who claim credit for the rescue, while the hero alone is recognized by the girl, marks this as essentially a popular tale. Rhŷs has pointed out (*Hib. Lect.*, pp. 342 ff.) that in one of Cuchulinn's expeditions to the Other World (preserved only in a fourteenth-century manuscript: see *Irische Texte*, II, i, 173–209) a giant has to be fought. Cuchulinn goes in a mysterious boat belonging to the Prince of Alban to a beautiful island surrounded by a wall of silver and a palisade of bronze, where he is entertained. He is directed to an adjoining island, where he encounters the giant Coirpre. After a long battle, the giant is overcome. He thereupon becomes very hospitable, brings Cuchulinn to his house, and bestows on him his daughter.

By good fortune, moreover, there is another ancient fairy-mistress story told of Cuchulinn, in which an exact parallel to the incident of Laudine's speedy marriage to the slayer of her husband appears. It is therefore certain that a development similar to that just assumed had actually taken place among the Celts before the time of Chrétien. The story occurs in a *Dinnshenchas* which gives only the summary of an ancient tale, rationalized so as to read like history. It runs in brief as follows [1]:

THE TALE OF CUROI.

Curoi mac Dairi's wife Bláthnat, daughter of Menn, king of Falga, loved Cuchulinn and urged him to come and take her from Curoi. Cuchulinn did so. At an appointed signal, he stormed the fort, slew its owner, and married Bláthnat. Together with her he secured the famous cows and cauldron belonging to Curoi.

Falga is glossed in the manuscript "the Hebrides of to-day," [2] but there can be no doubt that it was a synonym for the Other World.[3] It is sometimes identified with the Isle of Man,[4] which, as we noted when treating of Manannán, was confused by the ancient Celts with the Land beyond the Waves. Menn (or Mider), king of the Isle of Man (or Fairyland), is well known.[5] It is clear, then, that Bláthnat was a *fée*.

Curoi, her husband, is an exactly parallel figure to Manannán mac Lir.[6] He is a magician and shape-shifter, and also Lord of

---

[1] *Facsimile of the Book of Leinster*, 169, β, 42 ff. Printed by O'Grady, *Silva Gadelica*, II, 482 (translation at p. 530).

[2] "Inse Gall indiu" (LL, 169, β, 46).

[3] It is so used in the Bodley *Dinnshenchas* (see Nutt, *Voyage of Bran*, I, 213, and *Folk Lore*, III, 471).

[4] Henderson, *Fled Bricrend*, p. 142; Rhŷs, *Hib. Lect.*, p. 476.

[5] He so appears in the *Tochmarc Etáine* in the *Lebor na h-Uidre*, edited by Windisch, *Irische Texte*, I, 127 ff.; cf. I, 204, note.

[6] O'Grady, *Hist. of Ireland*, p. 220, note (cited by Henderson, *Fled Bricrend*, p. 195), views Curoi "as the great Southern marine genius, corresponding to Manannán amongst the Northern Irish." Henderson (p. 197) calls him "a great magician, really an Other-World power, at any rate a water-demon like Grendel."

the Sea. His combat with Cuchulinn is referred to in an ancient Welsh poem, *Marwnat Corroi map Dayry,*[1] which shows that his story was famous among the Brythonic as well as the Goidelic Celts.

---

[1] No. xlii in the *Book of Taliessin,* a manuscript considered by Skene (*Four Books,* I, 3) to belong to the beginning of the fourteenth century. The text is printed by Skene, II, 198, with a translation, I, 254–255. I quote a more recent translation by Rhŷs in *Proc. of Roy. Soc. of Ant. of Ireland,* XXI, 642 ff. (1891).

A LAMENT FOR CORROI.

Thy broad fountain replenishes the world:
It comes, it goes, it hurries to Dover.
The death-wail of Corroi has startled me;
Cold the deed of him of rugged passions,
Whose crime was one which few have heard of.
Daire's son held a helm on the Southern Sea,
Sung was his praise before his burial.
Thy broad fountain replenishes Nonneu:
It comes, it goes, it hurries to Dover;
But mine is the death-wail of Corroi;
Cold the deed of him of rugged passions,
Whose crime was one that few have heard of.

Thy broad fountain replenishes thy tide,
Thine arrow speeds for the . . . strand of Dover,
Subjugator, vast is thy battle-front,
And after Man it is to the towns
They go . . . of Gwinionydd.
Whilst victorious the space of . . . morning
News I am told of men on the ground,
The adventures of Corroi and Cuchulainn,
Of many a turmoil on their frontier,
Whilst the head of a gentle host was . . .
The noble fort that falls not nor quakes.
Blessed is the soul that meant it.

Instead of "Daire's son held a helm," etc., Skene translates, "Mac Daire, lord of the southern sea." In any case, it is plain that the poem calls the ocean Curoi's "broad fountain," which is enough to mark him as a kind of sea-divinity. It is fair to add that O'Curry, *Manners and Customs,* III, 81, quotes a story that represents Cuchulinn as having in the first place carried off Bláthnat from her father Mider; Curoi stole her from him, and therefore Cuchulinn, in slaying the latter, was only regaining his rights. Even if this be a part of the old tale, it in no way modifies any conclusions reached above. Curoi is as surely an Other-World king as Mider.

Curoi appears in the Irish *Fled Bricrend*[1] as a magician dwelling in a revolving castle beside a loch. The three champions of Ulster

---

[1] Edited by Henderson, from the *Lebor na h-Uidre* and later manuscripts. The story, like most of the texts in LU, shows evidence of having been compiled from various older sources. Henderson says (p. xliv): "One is assuredly right in holding that a tale like the Emain-Curoi story was current in Erin during the last quarter of the ninth century. For anything to the contrary I see no reason why, in the main essentials, it should not *orally* go back to the earliest period of Irish Saga." The story is, that, — at the feast given by Bricriu, — Loigaire, Conall, and Cuchulinn fell to quarrelling as to which should have the Hero's Portion. They were directed to go to Curoi mac Dairi:

"'He will adjudge ye truly. To ask him demandeth courage.'"

Loigaire set out first. When he approached the place, "a dim, dark, heavy mist overtook him, confusing him in such wise that it was impossible for him to fare farther on the way." A huge giant now appeared and overthrew him, robbing him of his horses, his chariot, and his arms.

"Not long thereafter Conall the Victorious took the same way and arrived at the plain where the druidical mist overtook Loigaire." The like hideous, black, dark cloud overtook him, and he fared in the same way at the hands of the giant.

Cuchulinn then set out, and overthrew the giant, bringing back with him his own horses and arms, as well as those of his fellows. [It is not said that the giant is Curoi, but as they set out to go to Curoi it is natural to suppose that they found him.] His two rivals still refused to yield Cuchulinn the championship. After another quarrel, the three heroes are told to go to the ford of Yellow, son of Fair. "He will adjudge ye." Yellow felt that the task was too difficult. "But I know," he added, "one who will venture it, viz., Terror, son of Great Fear . . . , at yonder loch." Off then in quest of him they went. Terror was "a big powerful fellow. . . . He used to shift his form into what shape he pleased, was wont to do tricks of magic and such like arts. He in sooth was the wizard from whom Muni, the Wizard's pass, is named. [This reminds one of Rhŷs's connection of Manannán with *mon-*: see p. 42, note.] He used to be called wizard from the extent to which he changed his divers shapes."

Terror proposed the beheading game. He allowed Loigaire to cut off his head, picked the head up and went with it into his loch. On the morrow the giant returned, but Loigaire shirked his part of the bargain. The same was true of Conall, but Cuchulinn stood the test. Terror spared him and awarded him the supremacy, because he did not shrink.

As soon, however, as the heroes had returned to the palace, "Loigaire and Conall disputed the verdict given in favor of Cuchulinn. . . . The Ultonians advised them to go for judgment unto Curoi. To that too they agreed." They set off for Fort Curoi, where they were entertained by Bláthnat, Mind's daughter,

betook themselves to his mysterious fort to secure his decision as to which was the greatest warrior. He knew beforehand of their coming (as is always the case in the Other-World journey) and arranged

---

wife of Curoi. "That night on their arrival Curoi was not at home. But knowing they would come, he counselled his wife regarding the heroes."

When bedtime came, she told them that each was to take his night, watching the fort until Curoi should return. "In what airt soever of the globe Curoi should happen to be, every night o'er the fort he chaunted a spell, till the fort revolved as swiftly as a mill-stone. The entrance was never to be found after sunset." Loigaire was sentry the first night. He was attacked by a monstrous giant from the sea, who tossed him out over the wall of the fort into the mire of the ditch. The second night Conall fared in the same way.

The third night Cuchulinn kept watch. First he was attacked by twenty-seven warriors, whom he slew one after another. Then the monster of the loch came towards the fort "opening its mouth so that one of the palaces could go into its gullet." Cuchulinn dispatched it. "Then a giant approached westwards from the sea." Cuchulinn overcame him, and only spared his life on condition that he grant him the sovereignty of Erin's heroes. "It shall be thine," quoth the giant, who thereupon vanished, he knew not whither. Cuchulinn then by a tremendous effort sprang over the wall of the fort, as he supposed his fellows to have done. When he had entered the house " Bláthnat made speech : 'Truly, not the sigh of one dishonored but a victor's sigh of triumph,'" for she knew full well the struggle Cuchulinn had had that night. It was not long when they beheld Curoi coming towards them. He complimented Cuchulinn, and assigned to him the sovereignty. The heroes thereupon returned to Emain.

But Cuchulinn's superiority was again disputed ; whereupon, as the Ultonians were assembled, an ugly black giant entered the hall. He was clad in an old hide and had ravenous yellow eyes protruding from his head, each the size of an ox-vat. In his left hand he carried a club, a burden for twenty yoke of oxen, and in his right hand an axe. He proposed the beheading game, in which Loigaire and Conall were found wanting. [Here the ancient manuscript (LU) breaks off. The remainder of the tale is supplied from a fifteenth-century manuscript, which agrees so perfectly with what precedes that it must be regarded as authentic.] Cuchulinn does not flinch when his turn comes to put his head on the block. The giant, however, merely taps him with the blunt side of the axe and exclaims :

"O Cuchulinn, arise ! The sovereignty of the heroes of Erin is thine henceforth."

" Then the giant vanished. It was Curoi mac Dairi who had come in that guise to fulfill the promise he had given to Cuchulinn."

The present form of this story, with its many repetitions, has probably, as Henderson suggests, resulted from the addition of several variants of what was at

for them a warm reception. The failure of Loigaire and of Conall is contrasted with the success of Cuchulinn after a tremendous combat in which he won a compliment from Curoi's wife Bláthnat [1] (very much as in the *Ivain* the failure of Calogrenant is set off against the

---

bottom the same tale. Certainly, Terror, son of Great Fear, seems to be a mere variant of Curoi. He does the same things, and like Curoi is a water demon. He dives into the loch so that, like Fiachna in the *Tale of Loegaire*, his home must be beneath the waves. Furthermore, "Terror" can hardly be his real name. He is probably Curoi in disguise.

Whether this be so or not, I do not see how there can be any reasonable doubt that the giant whom Cuchulinn overcomes at Curoi's fort and compels to promise him the sovereignty, is Curoi in one of his magic shapes. Curoi has purposely absented himself just before the arrival of the heroes, and he returns directly after the sudden vanishing of the giant. What more natural than that he should himself test the heroes, just as we are expressly told that he did in the beheading game? Furthermore, if the giant is not Curoi, how can he promise the sovereignty, inasmuch as Cuchulinn is sworn to abide by the decision of Curoi?

If this explanation be correct, the kind words of praise bestowed by Bláthnat on Cuchulinn when he proves himself victor over her husband are significant. The *Fled Bricrend* may preserve another form of the tale of which the LL *Dinnshenchas* gives a euhemerized account. There is a combat in both, though only the *Dinnshenchas* represents Curoi as slain. But the killing of the husband would naturally be omitted in the *Fled Bricrend*, where it is needful to have Curoi come to the court at Emain in person in order to assign permanently the sovereignty to Cuchulinn.

It is interesting to compare a modern Irish tale in which Cuchulinn by overcoming a giant and entering a revolving castle wins a fairy mistress (see Curtin, *Myths and Folk-Lore of Ireland*, pp. 304–326). Cucúlin, as his name is here spelled, is represented as one of the champions of Finn mac Cool. He is persuaded to the adventure by the fairy herself, whose name is Gil an Og (Water of Life). She comes to the court of Finn with a magic shirt that would fit no one but Cucúlin. She also presents him with a marvellous speckled boat, in which to journey to the scene of the adventure. Cucúlin is obliged to overcome a *gruagach*, who lives in an island surrounded by a chain and a ring of fire seven miles wide. He has also to slay a creature called "Thin-in-Iron" and to enter a turning castle that has but one door, before he finally wins the hand of Gil an Og. "Thin-in-Iron" may plausibly be regarded as a magician in disguise, and therefore as a parallel figure to Curoi.

[1] Zimmer rightly interprets this as meaning that Cuchulinn alone could force his way to the under world: "Hierin liegt wol, dass Cuchulinn ursprünglich allein in die unterwelt vordrang" (*Zt. f. deutsches Alt.*, XXXII, 331).

success of the hero). One of Curoi's disguises in this story is the form of a black giant whom not even beheading can kill.

Keeping clear of theory, it is plain from a comparison of this ancient account with that in the *Dinnshenchas* in LL, that Cuchulinn was credited with an Other-World Journey, in which he slew a giant who dwelt in a revolving castle, and married the giant's fairy wife. No closer parallel to the incidents of Laudine's marriage to Iwain could be found. The situation in the *Matron of Ephesus*, which has been put forward as a close parallel to the remarriage of Laudine, falls far short of this, for in it the lady *does not marry* the *slayer* of her husband, but only a soldier appointed to guard the corpses of some criminals. The *Matron of Ephesus* theory, whose only claim to attention was its supposed ability to explain this situation, is thus shown to break down utterly, even at the central point of its supposed strength.

CHAPTER IV (*Continued*).

ANCIENT CELTIC STORIES OF THE JOURNEY TO THE OTHER WORLD.

III. The Imrama.

The germ of the *imram* is found in the oldest Celtic fairy tales. Connla was carried off in a boat of glass. In the *Serglige* the hero was ferried over to Labraid's isle in a ship of bronze. The term *imram*, however, is generally reserved for a particular class of Other-World journeys, in which stress is laid on the incidents of a voyage by sea and on the number of islands visited. In the *Imram Mailduin*, the best example of the type, more than thirty islands are described.

The *imrama* have been built up, apparently by scribes, out of the material of older Other-World journeys like the *Echtra Condla*.[1] The

---

[1] Zimmer (*Zt. f. deutsches Alt.*, XXXIII, 129–220, 257–338) has shown that the *Navigatio Brendani*, and especially the earlier *imrama* (such as the *Mailduin*), are based essentially on ancient Celtic tradition and story concerning the Other World. From the Latin *Navigatio* there arose, as he points out, a vast literature in all European languages.

motive that seems to have determined the special form was a fond-
ness for variety of adventure.[1] The interest is centred, not, as in
the tales just discussed, on the struggle necessary to win the hand
of the *fée*, but on the strange incidents and dangers of the journey.
The *imrama* are essentially books of adventure.

Another motive that strongly affected the later *imrama*, and even
the *Voyage of Mailduin*, though it scarcely touched the *Voyage of
Bran*, was a desire to identify the Other World with Christian conceptions and thus to take advantage of the interest that Christians
have always manifested in visions of any sort relating to Paradise.
A word of explanation may be allowed here. It was a Christian
belief that the souls of certain just men had gone, not directly
to heaven, but to an intermediate place of happiness, there to abide
till the Day of Judgment. This region was commonly identified
with the Garden of Eden and thought of as containing the Tree of
Life and other familiar features of the landscape of Paradise. The
Celts, noticing a similarity between this place and their Happy
Other World, strove in their *imrama* to show that those heroes
who found their way to the Other World caught also glimpses of the
Earthly Paradise.[2] This is probably the explanation of the absence
of the combat motive from all the *imrama*, for evidently, if fighting
were pictured in the Other World, all chance of identifying it with
the Christian Paradise would be at an end.

The process of identification of the Other World with the Earthly
Paradise was a gradual one. The *Imram Brain* shows, as has been
said, hardly a trace of it, and is indeed scarcely an *imram* at all.
But two different islands are visited, and the incidents of the sea
voyage are not much dwelt on. It might almost as well be classed
with the Other-World journeys as with the *imrama*. This is an
important fact, as showing how idle it would be to hold that the

---

[1] Zimmer (l.c., p. 331) thinks the *imrama* were patterned in the first place
after Virgil's *Æneid*. They arose, he says, in the seventh and eighth centuries in
imitation of Æneas's voyage.

[2] Zimmer holds (l.c., p. 286) that the definite descriptions of the Earthly Paradise found in mediæval literature after the twelfth century are based largely on
Celtic conceptions of the Other World.

imrama could be essentially based on anything else than Celtic Other-World story.   The *Imram Brain* is, indeed, a connecting link between the Other-World Journey and the *imram*.

In the *Mailduin* the identification with the Earthly Paradise appears at several points.   It is rather clumsily done, however, so that it is plain that the great body of the tale must go back to Celtic story.   It is perfectly safe, therefore, to use the incidents in it, as well as those in the *Bran*, to throw light on the development which various themes found in the *Serglige* may have taken in Celtic literature before the time of Chrétien.

Besides the importance which the *Voyage of Bran* has as an illustration of the development of a journey into an *imram*, it is valuable also for the good description of the Other-World landscape that it contains.   The story is very briefly this :

IMRAM BRAIN MAIC FEBAIL.[1]

A woman, a messenger from an unknown land, mysteriously appeared in Bran's house one day when the doors were closed and the house was full of chiefs and princes.   She sang many verses describing her pleasant country (§ 1) :

> There is a distant isle
> Around which sea-horses glisten. . . .
> Lovely land throughout the world's age,
> On which the many blossoms drop (§ 4). . . .
> An ancient tree there is with blossoms,
> On which birds call to the Hours.[2]
> 'T is in harmony, it is their wont
> To call together every Hour (§ 7).

After inviting Bran to her land, the woman disappeared as suddenly as she had come (§ 31).

---

[1] Summarized from Kuno Meyer's translation, *The Voyage of Bran*, I, 1–35. Meyer has also edited the text (l.c., I, 1–35) from LU and later MSS. From considerations of language Meyer thinks (I, xvi) that it "was originally written down in the seventh century."   To this period it had been previously assigned by Zimmer (*Haupt's Zt.*, XXXIII, 261), though with some caution.   A summary of the tale is given by Zimmer (l.c., pp. 257–261).

[2] Meyer (p. 6) notes that this must mean "the canonical Hours" and be "an allusion to church music."

On the next day Bran chose his companions and put to sea. After sailing two days, they met Manannán mac Lir driving his chariot across the ocean, which was for him a flowery plain (§§ 32–33).

He, too, sang verses describing Mag Mell, which seems to lie beneath the waves :

> Rivers pour forth a stream of honey
> In the land of Manannán, son of Ler (§ 36). . . .
> Though but one chariot rider is seen,
> In Mag Mell of many flowers,
> There are many steeds on its surface,
> Though thou seest them not (§ 39). . . .
> Along the top of a wood has swum
> Thy coracle across ridges.
> There is a wood of beautiful fruit
> Under the prow of thy little skiff.
> A wood with blossom and fruit,
> On which is the vine's veritable fragrance;
> A wood without decay, without defect,
> On which are leaves of golden hue (§§ 42–43). . . .
> Emne with many hues of hospitality
> Thou wilt reach before the setting of the sun (§ 60).

After Bran parted from Manannán, he came to the Island of Laughter, where he lost one of his men, who landed and fell to laughing like the rest of the men on the island (§ 61).

It was not long thereafter when they reached the Land of Women. There each man was provided with a partner in the usual manner. They remained there, supplied with all that they could desire, for what seemed to them a year. Then homesickness seized some of the men, and they persuaded Bran to depart (§§ 62–63).

When their ship reached the shore of Ireland, they found that they had been gone for centuries (§ 64). One of the men leaped from the coracle, but, as soon as he touched the earth of Ireland, he fell into a heap of ashes, as though he had been in the earth for many hundred years.[1] To the

---

[1] This supernatural lapse of time in the Other World appears in many Celtic tales. See for example the *Echtra Nera*, edited and translated by Stokes, *Rev. Celt.*, X, 214 ff. It is preserved only in a fourteenth-century MS., but, as its title appears in the celebrated list of Irish tales in the *Book of Leinster* (p. 245, β, 32 ff.), and as internal evidence is in favor of its having taken shape in very rude times, it is probably as old as the majority of the tales preserved in the oldest MSS. The story is that Nera left his people at a feast and entered a fairy hill (*síd*).

people that assembled on the shore Bran told all his wanderings from the beginning until that time. And he wrote these quatrains in Ogam, and then bade them farewell. And from that hour his wanderings are not known (§§ 65–66).

It will be seen that this tale does not differ essentially from the *Echtra Condla.* Both seem to draw from the same storehouse of Celtic fancy. The only distinct trace of Christian influence appears in the description of the Other-World landscape, where birds are said to sing " to the [canonical] Hours."

In the *Imram Mailduin,* on the other hand, are found all the marks of the *imram* type. Older Celtic material has been worked up to form a tale of adventure comparable to those of other peoples :

IMRAM CURAIG MAILDUIN.[1]

Maelduin determined to set out on the sea to search for his father's murderers. He was directed by a druid to take seventeen companions only, but at the last moment his three foster-brothers, who had not been included in the seventeen, begged to accompany him. When refused, they threw themselves into the sea and swam after the vessel. Out of pity Maelduin received them into his boat, but he was soon punished for disobeying the druid's injunction, because, though he speedily found the murderers in an The Island of the island, he was not able to slay them. A storm suddenly Murderers. came up and drove Maelduin's boat into " the great boundless ocean " (§ 1).

The king of the *síd* assigned to him a single woman, with whom he dwelt and who conceived a son by him. After what seemed three days, he returned and found his people still around the same caldron, engaged in the same feast. He showed them the summer fruit of the *síd* in order to convince them of the truth of his tale, and then went back into the *síd,* " nor will he come out till the Day of Doom."

The supernatural lapse of time appears in the *Adventures of Teigue,* and in Walter Map's tale of Herla.

[1] Summarized and quoted from the text and translation of Whitley Stokes, *Rev. Celt.,* IX, 447–495 ; X, 50–95. The MS. for the greater part of the tale is LU. Zimmer (*Haupt's Zt.,* XXXIII, 148) holds that the tale took shape in the eighth or ninth century. The possibility of alterations and additions having been made as late as the beginning of the eleventh century is, however, to be admitted. For a French translation, see d'Arbois, *L'Épopée Celtique,* I, 449–500 ; for one in German, Zimmer, l.c., pp. 150 ff. Cf. Nutt, *Voyage of Bran,* I, 163 ff.

The Island of Enormous Ants.   The first island they came to was inhabited by enormous ants (§ 2).

Huge Birds.   In the next island was a row of trees, and many great birds on the trees. They slew and ate the birds (§ 3).

When they came to the next island, they saw therein a beast like a horse. The legs of a hound he had, with rough, sharp nails, and great was his joy at seeing them, for he longed to devour them and their boat (§ 4).

Horselike Monster.

Demons' Horses.   In the next island they found enormous nuts and the tracks of monster horses that had been eating them (§ 5).

Then they found an island having a great house, with a door above, and a door into the sea, and against that door there was a valve of stone. This valve was pierced by an aperture, through which the sea waves were flinging the salmon into the midst of the house. Maelduin and his men entered that house, and therein they beheld a testered bed for the chief of the house alone, and a bed for every three of his household, and food for every three before every bed, and a cup of glass on every vessel. So they dined off that food and liquor (§ 6).

Empty Banquet Hall.

At the next island they found a cluster of three apples at the end of a rod. For forty nights each of those apples sufficed them (§ 7).

Wondrous Fruit.

Thereafter they found another island, on which was "a huge beast," which raced round about the island swifter than, the wind (§ 8).

Racing Beast.

Then they found a lofty island on which "were many great animals like unto horses. Each of them would take a piece out of another's side, and carry it away with its skin and its flesh, so that out of their sides streams of crimson blood were breaking" (§ 9).

Fighting Horses.

In the next island were "many trees full fruited with great golden apples." The fruit was devoured in the day time by "red animals like swine" and in the night by birds. Maelduin collected all the apples that were there. "Alike did the apples forbid hunger and thirst from them" (§ 10).

Golden Apples.

Then they sighted an island "where stood a fort surrounded by a white, high rampart as if it were built of burnt lime, or as if it were all one rock of chalk. Great was its height from the sea: it all but reached the clouds. The fort was wide open. Round the rampart were great snow-white houses. When they entered the largest of these they saw no one there, save a small cat which was in the midst of the house, playing on the four stone pillars that were there." . . . After that

Treasure-House of the Cat.

they saw three rows on the wall of the house, consisting of brooches and neck torques and swords made of gold and silver. "A roasted ox moreover and a flitch in the midst of the house and great vessels of good, intoxicating liquor. 'Hath this been left for us?' saith Maelduin to the cat. It looked at him suddenly and began to play again. Then Maelduin recognised that it was for them that the dinner had been left. So they dined and drank and slept." When they were ready to go, Maelduin's third foster-brother took one of the necklaces. But he got no farther than the middle of the enclosure, for the cat followed and sprang "through him like a fiery arrow, and burnt him to ashes," and then went back till it was on its pillar. Maelduin soothed the cat with his words, and, setting the necklace again in its place, they departed (§ 11).

Black and White Island. They espied another island divided by a brazen palisade. All objects placed on one side of this became black, and those on the other side became white (§ 12).

Huge Herdsman. Then they came to an island in which was a great mountain, "and they purposed to go and view the island from it. Now when the Rhymer and Germán went to visit the mountain, they found before them a broad river, which was not deep. Into this river Germán dipped the handle of his spear, and at once it was consumed as if fire had burnt it.[1] So they went no further. Then they saw on the other side of the river great hornless oxen lying down, and a huge man sitting by them, then Germán after this struck his spear-shaft against his shield to frighten the oxen. 'Why dost thou frighten the silly calves?' saith that huge herdsman. 'Where are the dams of those calves?' saith Germán. 'They are on the other side of yonder mountain,' saith he. So they went thence" (§ 13).

Hideous Miller. Thereafter they found an island with a great hideous mill, wherein was a huge hideous miller (§ 14).

Magic Air. Then they came to the isle of wailing, where another of Maelduin's foster-brothers was lost. Four other companions who landed were directed by Maelduin not to look at the land or the air, and to put their garments round their noses and their mouths, and not to breathe the air of the island, lest they should be detained like the foster-brother (§ 15).

Then they came to a lofty island divided into four parts. "A maiden went to meet them . . . and gave them food. They likened it to cheese;

---

[1] In the Dutch poem *Walewein* there is a river of fire which has the appearance of water (see Paris, *Romania*, XII, 509).

and whatever taste was pleasing to any one he would find it therein. And
she dealt liquor to them . . . so that they slept. When
Hospitable Hostess.
they awoke they were in their boat at sea. Nowhere did
they see their island or their maiden" (§ 16).

Then they found an island that had a fortress with a brazen door and a
bridge of glass, and when they went upon this bridge they fell down back-
Island of the Chaste wards. A woman came out of the fortress, pail in hand,
Maiden. took water and returned to the fortress. " A housekeeper
for Maelduin," said his men, but she scorned them, and when they struck
the brazen door, it made a sweet soothing music, which sent them to sleep
till the morrow. Three days and three nights were they in that wise.
" On the fourth day the woman came to them, beautiful verily and wearing
a white mantle with a circlet of gold round her golden hair. Two sandals
of silver on her rosy feet. A brooch of silver with studs of gold in her
mantle and a filmy silken smock next her white skin." She greeted each
man by his name: " It is long since your coming here hath been known and
understood." She took them into the house, she gave them food, " every
savor that each desired he would find therein." His men urged Maelduin
to offer himself to her, and proposed to her that she should show affection
to him and sleep with him. But, saying that she knew not and had never
known what sin was, she left them, promising an answer for the morrow.
When they awoke, they were in their boat on a crag, and they saw not the
island nor the fortress, nor the lady, nor the place where they had
been (§ 17).

"As they went from that place they heard in the northeast a great cry
and chaunt, as it were a singing of psalms. That night and the next day
till none they were rowing that they might know what cry
Chanting Birds.
or chaunt they heard. They behold a high mountainous
island full of birds, black and dun and speckled, shouting and speaking
loudly " (§ 18).

The next island contained many trees and birds and a man whose cloth-
Trees and the Pil- ing was his hair. He said: " The birds which thou behold-
grim. est in the trees are the souls of my children and my kindred,
both men and women, who are yonder awaiting Doomsday " (§ 19).

The next island " had a golden rampart about it." Therein they saw a
man " whose raiment was the hair of his own body." There was also
a marvellous fountain, which on Friday and Wednesday
Magic Fountain.
yields water, on Sundays milk, but on feast-days wine.
They drank of this fountain, which " cast them into a heavy sleep till the
morrow " (§ 20).

Savage Smiths. Then they came to the island of the Savage Smiths, from which they fled (§ 21).

Sea of Glass. Then they voyaged over a sea resembling green glass. " Such was its purity that the gravel and sand of the sea were clearly visible through it " (§ 22).

Beast in Tree. " They afterwards put forth into another sea like a cloud, and it seemed to them that it would not support them or the boat. Then they beheld under the sea down below them roofed strongholds and a beautiful country. And they see a beast, huge, awful, monstrous, in a tree there, and a drove of herds and flocks round about the tree ; and beside the tree an armed man with shield and spear and sword. When he beheld yon huge beast that abode in the tree he goeth thence at once in flight. The beast stretched forth his neck out of the tree, and sets his head into the back of the largest ox of the herd and dragged it into the tree, and anon devours it in the twinkling of an eye. The flocks and the herdsman flee away at once " (§ 23).

Shouting People. Thereafter they found an island around which rose the sea, making vast cliffs of water all about it. " As the people of that country perceived them they set to screaming at them and saying : ' It is they ! It is they ! ' till they were out of breath " (§ 24).

Water Arch. Then they came to an island above which was an arch of water like a rainbow (§ 25).

Silver Column. " Thereafter they voyaged till they found a great silver column. . . . And not a single sod of earth was about it, but only the boundless ocean." From its summit hung a silver net, through a mesh of which the boat went under sail. And Diurán cut a piece from the net with his spear, saying: " I do this so that my tidings may be the more believed [when I reach Ireland] " (§ 26).

Subaqueous Door. " Then they see another island standing on a single pedestal,[1] to wit, one foot supporting it, . . . and they saw down in the base of the pedestal a closed door under lock. They understood that *that* was the way by which the island was entered " (§ 27).

---

[1] It is possible that these islands rising like a pedestal or like a wall (cf. § 11) were in the first place based on the exaggerated accounts of mariners. In *Le Tour du Monde*, supplement, *A Travers le Monde*, 5 nov., 1898, pp. 357–358, there is an account of an island called Rockall, which is situated in the Atlantic Ocean 295 kilometres from any land (the British Isles), which suggests the descriptions of the *imrama*. This island consists of a single rock, 75 metres around, which rises like a pillar from the sea. It does not occur in any charts before the seventeenth century.

After that they came to a large island, and there was a great plain therein, and on this a great table-land, heatherless but grassy and smooth. And near the sea was a fortress, large, high, and strong, and a great house therein, adorned, and with good couches. Seventeen grown-up girls were there preparing a bath. When the wanderers saw this Maelduin felt sure the bath was for them. But there rode up a dame with a bordered purple mantle, gold-embroidered gloves on her hands, on her feet adorned sandals. She alighted, entered the fortress, and went to bathe. One of the damsels then welcomed the seafarers. " ' Come into the court: the queen invites you.' So they entered the fort, and they all bathed. The queen sat on one side of the house and her seventeen girls about her. Maelduin sat on the other side, over against the queen, with his seventeen men around him." Food and drink were served to them, and at nightfall the eighteen couples paired off, Maelduin sleeping with the queen. On the morrow she urged them to stay : " Age will not fall on you but the age that ye have attained. And lasting life ye shall have always : and what came to you last night shall come to you every night without any labour." Maelduin asked who she was, and she answered " wife of the king of the island, to whom she had borne seventeen daughters ; at her husband's death she had taken the kingship of the island ; and unless she go to judge the folk every day what happened the night before would not happen again." Maelduin and his men stayed three months, " and it seemed to them that those three months were three years." The men murmured and urged Maelduin to depart, and reproached him with the love he bore the queen, and one day, when she was at the judging, they took out the boat and would sail off. But she rode after them, and flung a clew which Maelduin caught, and it cleaved to his hand ; by this means she drew them back to land. Thrice this happened, and the men accused Maelduin of catching the clew purposely. He told off another man to mind the clew, whose hand, when touched by it, was cut off by one of the seafarers. So in that wise they escaped (§ 28).

The Isle of Maidens.

Then they came to an island with trees bearing marvellous berries. Maelduin drank some of the juice of the berries, which threw him into a deep sleep till the morning. He said : " Gather ye this fruit, for great is its excellence " (§ 29).

Trees with Berries.

Then they landed on an island where was a wood of yews and great oaks. Here they found great herds of sheep, a church, and an ancient cleric. Here, too, they saw an ancient eagle renewing its youth by bathing in a lake. Diurán also bathed in the lake, and he never suffered weakness or infirmity from that time forth so long as he lived (§ 30).

Lake of Youth.

Island of Laughter. Then they came to the Isle of Laughter, where the last of Maelduin's three foster-brothers was lost (§ 31).

"After that they sighted another island, which was not large, and a fiery rampart was round about it, and that rampart used to revolve round the island. There was an open doorway in the side of the

Fiery Revolving Rampart. rampart. Now whenever the doorway would come in its revolution opposite to them, they used to see the whole island, and all that was therein, and all its indwellers, even human beings, beautiful, abundant, wearing adorned garments, and feasting with golden vessels in their hands." And the wanderers listened to their ale-music (§ 32).

Then they came to the island of the hermit of Torach (§ 33).

They followed the direction in which they saw a falcon fly, and at length they sighted land like the land of Ireland. It was the small island on which they had found the murderers at the first. But Maelduin was now reconciled to them, and he returned to his own district in Ireland and declared his adventures (§ 34).

It has seemed necessary to outline very fully this charming voyage story, in order to bring out with fairness its curious character. Some incidents are plainly drawn from Christian tradition,[1] but in the case of only one island (§ 19) is there a definite attempt made at identification with the Earthly Paradise where the souls of the just await the Day of Judgment. The Christian and pagan materials are not thoroughly worked together, and it is easy to see, by comparison with the older Celtic tales already studied, that most of the material comes straight, as Zimmer thinks, from the mass of Irish Other-World lore. A study of this *imram*, therefore, ought to throw light on the development which the various incidents of the Other-World journey may have taken before the time of Chrétien.

In the *Imram Mailduin*, the idea of a single expedition to the Other World and return, as in the *Imram Brain* and in all the older stories, has been lost sight of. The compiler has either attached together several already existing variants of the same story, or else he or some preceding transcriber has divided up the adventures of a single Journey of Wonders, and the furniture of a single Other

---

[1] Traces of Christian influence appear in §§ 18, 19, 20, 30, 33, and 34.

World, among a number of different islands,[1] with the object of increasing the number of different adventures in his story. This point has been already made by Alfred Nutt, who sees a visit to the Other World not only in § 28 (The Isle of Maidens) but in § 17 (The Isle of the Chaste Maiden), which is, he maintains, a variant of the same episode. He also finds part of the gear of the Other World elsewhere in the story, and concludes that we are justified in making use of the several versions to recover the " original idea of Damsel Land as it existed in the material from which our story was drawn." He sees in § 32 (The Isle of the Fiery Revolving Rampart), for example, a part of the Other-World incident. It is tolerably clear, I think, that §§ 6 and 11 ought to be added to this list. In § 6 (The Empty Banquet Hall) we have a palace in which food is served by invisible means, — a well-established form of the Other-World story.[2] In § 11 (The Treasure-House of the Cat) there is the same empty palace, but it is guarded by a mysterious cat.

It is interesting to find the several repetitions of the Other-World story (§§ 6, 11, 17, 28, 32) arranged at tolerably equal intervals in the order of islands visited. This can be conveniently shown by placing the successive incidents in parallel columns as on pp. 68, 69.

A glance at this arrangement of the incidents of the *Mailduin* will show that, as § 28 is the longest and most characteristic description of the Other World, so, too, the adventures leading up to this capital episode are the most numerous and the most detailed. It appears, therefore, that this part of the tale (§§ 18–28) is either the original kernel of the whole, or else perhaps the most complete of several variants which have been put together to make up that whole. The incidents of this portion of the *Mailduin* should therefore form a basis for comparison.

If, now, we compare column IV with columns I, II, III, and V, a certain parallelism is discoverable. In all of the columns, except

---

[1] The manner in which a new island is brought in at every turn suggests the invention of a single transcriber who had a new idea and developed it *con amore* in the mediæval manner.

[2] Connla was promised "perpetual feasts without preparation," and at Labraid's isle in the *Serglige* there was a never-failing cask of mead.

I		II		III	
§ 1.	Island of the Murderers.				
§ 2.	Enormous Ants.	§ 7.	Wondrous Fruit.		
§ 3.	Huge Birds.				
				§ 12.	Black and White Isle.
		§ 8.	Racing Beast.		
§ 4.	Horselike Monster.	§ 9.	Fighting Horses.	§ 13.	Huge Herdsman.
§ 5.	Demons' Horses.			§ 14.	Hideous Miller.
		§ 10.	Golden Apples.	§ 15.	Magic Air.
				§ 16.	Hospitable Hostess.
§ 6.	Empty Banquet Hall.	§ 11.	Treasure-House of the Cat.	§ 17.	Isle of the Chaste Maiden.

III, marvellous birds or trees are encountered. In all, except column V, fighting beasts of one kind or another appear. In several of the columns, a difficult passage of some kind, such as a subaqueous door or a revolving rampart, is described. It is natural to conclude that these three themes, which recur over and over again in different shapes, must have been, like the love-making motive, stock incidents of the Celtic Other-World Journey. Otherwise it is not easy to explain why the compiler of this *imram* should have introduced them in so many forms.

The first of these three themes may be called that of the Other-World Landscape. We have already met it in the *Serglige* and in the *Imram Brain*. The "great chaunt of birds," in § 18, "as it were a-singing psalms," reminds us of the birds calling to the canonical Hours in the *Imram Brain*. Much light is thrown on this incident by § 19, where are described trees full of birds that are the souls of men. It is absurd to find ordinary birds singing psalms, but for transformed souls this would be natural. We may be sure, therefore, that the birds in § 18 were originally one with those in § 19, and, like them, souls in bird shape. The separation must have been made by a stupid transcriber, anxious to increase the number of islands visited. In § 20 there is a marvellous fountain which yields milk on Sundays. Of course it is here a Christian marvel, but if we remember the "noble well" hard by the tree with singing birds in

IV	V
§ 18. The Chanting Birds.	
§ 19. The Trees and the Pilgrim.	§ 29. Trees with Magic Fruit.
§ 20. Magic Fountain.	§ 30. Lake of Youth.
§ 21. Savage Smiths.	
§ 22. The Sea of Glass.	
§ 23. The Beast in the Tree.	
§ 24. Shouting People.	§ 31. The Isle of Laughter.
§ 25. The Water Arch.	
§ 26. The Silver Column.	
§ 27. Subaqueous Door.	
§ 28. The Isle of Maidens.	§ 32. The Revolving Rampart.

the *Serglige*, it seems certain that this Christian fountain has been substituted for the Other-World Fountain. Making proper allowances, therefore, for the way in which the transcriber of this *imram* has divided up his material, we see in the scenery of these three islands a parallel to the tree with birds who do " lor servise " beside the Fountain Perilous in the *Ivain*.

The beast-like herdsman guarding cattle, in § 23 of the *Mailduin*, suggests the giant herdsman of the *Ivain*.

The third motive, that of the Perilous Passage, appears, as has been said, in the subaqueous door, in the revolving rampart, and, it may be added, in the brazen door of § 17, which, when struck, put Maelduin's men to sleep. It may be suggested that this danger, just at the entrance of the Other World, has been rationalized into the falling gates of the *Ivain*.

It is clear from what has been said that we have in the *imrama* important materials for the study of the Other-World Journey. For convenience, the different motives just outlined will be taken up one by one. Perhaps that of the Giant Herdsman should be discussed first, since it seems not to have been preserved except in the *imrama*.

CHAPTER IV (*Continued*).

ANCIENT CELTIC STORIES OF THE JOURNEY TO THE
OTHER WORLD.

IV. THE GIANT HERDSMAN MOTIVE.

IT will be remembered that, in the *Ivain*,[1] Calogrenant, after part-
ing from the Hospitable Host, came upon wild and savage bulls
fighting with such fierceness in the forest that he was fain to draw
back and avoid them.   He encountered, however, a monstrous and
hideous churl, who resembled a Moor, and was so ugly, in fact, that
he could not be described.   This creature sat on a stump, holding a
great club in his hand.   He had a head larger than that of a horse
and mossy ears the size of an elephant's.   He had the eyes of an
owl, the nose of a cat, his mouth was cleft like that of a wolf, and
his boar's teeth were sharp and red.   He leaned on his club and
did not speak to Calogrenant any more than a beast would do.
His only movement, as Calogrenant approached, was to mount upon
a tree trunk.   Naturally Calogrenant's first words to this creature
were to ask him what he was.   He replied that he was a man and
was guarding these beasts of the forest.   Calogrenant expressed
doubts about any man's being able to control such savage creatures.
The monster replied that he could seize one of the bulls by the horns
in such a way that all the others would tremble for fear and would
gather round as if to implore mercy; in this way he controlled the
beasts.   Calogrenant then asked the giant herdsman to direct him
to some adventure.   The herdsman obligingly described the adventure of the Fountain Perilous and showed the path that led thither.

This strange episode is plainly not the invention of Chrétien.[2]
No one, however, has before pointed out exactly why it appears in

---

[1] *Ivain*, vv. 278–409.

[2] So Baist has expressed himself (*Zt. f. rom. Phil.*, XXI, 402–405). He has,
moreover, compared § 13 of the *Mailduin*, but he has not noticed the parallels in
§§ 4, 5, 9, and 23, nor has he explained how this adventure came to find its way
into the *Ivain*.

the *Ivain.* I believe it to have been a stock incident of the Other-World Journey. The object of the giant herdsman is to point out the way to the Other World, i.e. to Laudine's castle. Chrétien has retained, almost without attempt at rationalization, one of the adventures of the type of Celtic story that we are studying. It is true that this theme does not occur in the *Serglige*, the norm for our comparisons, but it has left so many traces in the *Imram Mailduin* that we may feel confident that it was a stock incident.

The distinctive features of this adventure in the *Ivain* may be summed up thus : (1) a hideous beast-like giant, (2) who is perched upon a tree trunk, (3) is guarding a herd of animals. These (4) are not ordinary cattle, but savage beasts who fight each other arrogantly; yet (5) the monster herdsman is able to seize any one of them in a terrible way. (6) He points out to the traveller the road to a marvellous land.

In § 23 of the *Mailduin*, there is an adventure which unites features 1, 2, 3, and 5, and thus forms a striking parallel to the *Ivain:* "a beast, huge, awful, monstrous, in a tree, and a drove of herds and flocks round about the tree." "The beast stretched forth his neck out of the tree, and set his head into the back of the largest ox of the herd and dragged it into the tree and anon devoured it in the twinkling of an eye." [1] It is to be noted that this creature is seen in the Land beneath the Waves, that is, in the Other World.

---

[1] Compare the description of the herdsman in the *Ivain* (vv. 288 ff.):

> Un vilain qui resanbloit mor,
> Grant et hideus a desmesure
> (Einsi tres leide creature,
> Qu'an ne porroit dire de boche),
> Vi je seoir sor une çoche,
> Une grant maçue an sa main.
> Je m'aprochai vers le vilain,
> Si vi qu'il ot grosse la teste
> Plus que roncins ne autre beste,
> Chevos meschiez et front pelé,
> S'ot plus de deus espanz de le,
> Oroilles mossues et granz
> Auteus com a uns olifanz,
> Les sorciz granz et le vis plat,
> Iauz de choete et nes de chat,

To this incident of § 23 (in column IV) there is so striking a parallel in § 13 (column III) that we cannot doubt that they are variants of the same motive. In § 23 there are parallels to features 1, 3, and 6 of the adventure in the *Ivain*. The herdsman is here described as "a huge man" guarding "great hornless oxen." He gives the travellers information about the way, just as the Giant Herdsman directs Calogrenant and Iwain. Here again the creature

> Boche fandue come los,
> Danz de sangler aguz et ros,
> Barbe noire, grenons tortiz,
> Et le manton aers au piz,
> Longue eschine, toite et boçue. . . .
> Et fu montez desor un tronc,
> S'ot bien dis et set piez de lonc ;
> Si m'esgarda et mot ne dist
> Ne plus qu'une beste feïst ;
> Et je cuidai que il n'eüst
> Reison ne parler ne seüst.

That the herdsman was as much like a beast as a man is apparent, not only from this description, but from the reflections of Iwain (vv. 794 ff.):

> Si vit les tors et le vilain
> Qui la voie li anseigna ;
> Mes plus de çant foiz se seigna
> De la mervoille que il ot,
> Comant Nature feire sot
> Oevre si leide et si vilainne.

The fact that the guardian of the herd is called a "beast" in the *Mailduin* does not therefore injure the parallel.

It is not said in the *Ivain* that the creature could devour one of his cattle, but his description of his own powers is not unlike the words of the *Mailduin* (vv. 344 ff.):

> N'i a celi qui s'ost movoir
> Des qu'eles me voient venir.
> Car quant j'an puis une tenir,
> Si la destraing par les deus corz
> As poinz que j'ai et durs et forz,
> Que les autres de peor tranblent
> Et tot anviron moi s'asanblent
> Aussi con por merci crïer ;
> Ne nus ne s'i porroit fïer
> Fors moi, s'antr'eles s'estoit mis,
> Que maintenant ne fust ocis.
> Einsi sui de mes bestes sire.

seems to be in the Other World. He is beyond a river that burns anything dipped in it as if it were a stream of fire.

Having thus found variants of this motive in two[1] of the columns (III and IV) of our *Mailduin* table, we are perhaps justified in regarding the fighting beasts of columns I and II as indistinct survivals or variants of the same theme. In §§ 4 and 5 (column I) are described monstrous beasts "like horses, having the legs of a hound with rough sharp nails." They are evidently ferocious, like the bulls in the *Ivain*,[2] for "they long to devour the travellers and their boat."

A closer parallel, however, to the fighting bulls of the *Ivain* is found in § 9 (column II), where the travellers see "many great animals like unto horses" which were fighting each other. "Each would take a piece out of another's side, and carry it away with its skin and its flesh, so that out of their sides streams of crimson blood were breaking." In this account and that in column I the animals are described as "horselike." Their actions, however, are not those of horses, and probably this adjective does not mark them off significantly from the cattle of §§ 13 and 23.

The six distinguishing features of the Giant Herdsman motive in the *Ivain* are thus all found in the older *Imram Mailduin*. They do not

---

[1] That this method of operation is justified will, I think, be admitted by any one who studies the case of what I have called the Other-World landscape motive. From the fact that singing birds appear in § 18 of the *Mailduin*, a marvellous tree in § 19, and a magic fountain in § 20, it was conjectured that these three features must (in the more primitive Other-World tales from which the *Mailduin* has been built up) have been united to form one landscape like that in the *Serglige*. This at first thought somewhat daring process turns out to be entirely justified, for in the *Navigatio Brendani*, which must go back to Celtic *imrama*, these three features, the birds, the tree, and the fountain, *are* found united in exactly the way assumed.

[2] The description in the *Ivain* runs thus (vv. 280 ff.) :

> Tors sauvages et espaarz
> Qui s'antrecombatoient tuit
> Et demenoient si grant bruit
> Et tel fierté et tel orguel,
> Se le voir conter vos an vuel,
> Que de paor me tres arriere ;
> Que nule beste n'est plus fiere
> Ne plus orguelleuse de tor.

all, to be sure, occur united in one incident, but enough of them are found so joined to make the parallel hold good. Everything, therefore, seems to indicate that this is a stock episode of the Celtic Other-World Journey,[1] which has been preserved by Chrétien in his *Ivain*, with but little change from its more primitive form.

---

[1] An illustration of this character of the incident seems to be found in the *Echtra Thaidg mheic Chein*, an Irish Other-World tale preserved only in a fifteenth-century MS. I will summarize this tale, utilizing O'Grady's translation, *Silva Gadelica*, II, 385–401 (text, I, 343–359):

Teigue and his companions came to an island where they found no signs of human habitation, but only flocks of sheep. "The size of these creatures was unutterable; they were not less than horses of the largest [kind]." "One parlous great flock in particular they found there, of gigantic rams [of] which a single special one exceeded all: nine horns bedecked him, and on the heroes he charged violently butting." Teigue and his men had a battle with these rams. [It is possible, of course, that the likeness between these animals and those of the *Mailduin* is due to chance; but, as these beasts are described as horselike and as fierce creatures engaged in fighting, it is likely that we have here traces of the motive found in the *Mailduin* and in the *Ivain*.]

After leaving this island, Teigue and his men came to a beautiful land where it was summer, though at that time it was winter in Ireland. "Extraordinary was the amenity of the spot to which they now attained, but they left it and happened on a wood. Great was the excellence of its scent. Round purple berries hung on it . . . Birds, beautiful, brilliant, feasted on these grapes. As they fed they warbled music and minstrelsy, that was melodious and superlative, to which patients of every kind and the repeatedly wounded would have fallen asleep."

Going on from this spot, they found on the first hill "a white-bodied lady," "the fairest of the world's women"; on the second hill "a queen of gracious form draped in a vesture of golden fabric," and on the third hill a noble pair, a youth and a maid. It was Connla, son of Conn of the Hundred Battles, and the maid was "the young woman of many charms" that brought him hither. Connla "held in his hand a fragrant apple having the color of gold; a third part of it he would eat and still, for all he consumed, never a whit would it be diminished. This fruit it was that supported the pair of them, and when once they had partaken of it neither age nor dimness could affect them." They now entered "a jocund house with a silver floor." "Gems of crystal and carbuncle were set in the wall in such wise that with flashing of these precious stones day and night alike were bright there." "Then three birds enter to them into the house and perch on the thickly-furnished, wide-spreading apple tree that was in the court of the house. The birds eat an apple apiece and warble melody and harmony such that the sick would sleep to it." At length Teigue spoke of returning

CHAPTER IV (*Continued*).

ANCIENT CELTIC STORIES OF THE JOURNEY TO THE
OTHER WORLD.

V. THE PERILOUS PASSAGE.

IN the *Serglige* there was a perilous passage on the way to Labraid's isle. Fand declared to Loeg that he would not escape alive unless a woman protected him; therefore, we are told, Liban put her hand on his shoulder. There are in the *Mailduin* many indications that a dangerous passage of some kind must have been a stock incident of the Other-World journey. When the voyagers came to the Island of the Chaste Maiden (§ 17), which is, as has been pointed out, a variant of an original Other-World episode, they found a bridge of glass and a bronze door. Whoever stepped upon the bridge of glass fell backward,[1] and whoever struck the brazen door was put to sleep till the morrow by the sweet music that it made. After two days of vain attempt the travellers are escorted through this mysterious passage by a woman.[2]

---

to his land. "These birds will go with you," said the lady. "They will give you guidance and make you symphony and minstrelsy, and till again ye reach Ireland neither by land nor by sea shall sadness or grief afflict you." They thought they had been in the island but a day. They found that it had been a year. They set sail, and after some adventures returned to Ireland.

[1] Cuchulinn on his way to Scáthach's abode (Scáthach, "the shadowy one," is evidently an Other-World creature) had to pass a bridge that was low at both ends, high in the middle, and so constructed that when a man stepped on the one end the other end would rise aloft, and he would be thrown down. See Rhŷs, *Hib. Lect.*, p. 451, quoting from the *Tochmarc Emere*, and Hall, *Cuchullin Saga*, p. 75. This is a variant of the well-known "Bridge of Dread" motive.

[2] Rhŷs, *Arthurian Legend*, p. 303, has not noticed this parallel, but he has compared the passage in the *Serglige* with Peredur's entrance into a revolving castle in the Welsh *Seint Greal* (ed. Williams, pp. 325–326; translation, p. 649). Peredur is escorted into this castle by a damsel, who goes before him, carrying his shield and his spear, to warrant him. This same incident, of course, is found in the prose *Perceval* (ed. Potvin, I, 196), and may possibly be a survival of the

The locked and apparently subaqueous door in *Mailduin* (§ 27) has been spoken of. It was seen just before the travellers reached the Isle of Maidens or the Happy Other World. When one recollects that in the *Tale of Loegaire* entrance to the Other World was effected by diving into the loch, and that Terror in *Fled Bricrend*, who is a mere duplicate of Curoi, departed after the head-cutting contest into the loch, it seems likely that we have in this door a surviving trace of a perilous under-water passage.[1]

Obviously the revolving rampart of fire in *Mailduin* (§ 32), through a doorway in which, whenever it came opposite to them, the voyagers could see a land of marvellous splendor, is a variant of the Perilous-Passage motive. The beauty of the inhabitants seen within, their adorned garments, their perpetual feasting from golden vessels, and their far-prevailing music make the Other-World character of the place unmistakable. The revolving castle of the *Fled Bricrend*, in which Curoi lived with his wife Bláthnat, must also be regarded, as has been said, as an Other-World fortress. There are, then, in the most ancient Irish documents, two clear cases of the attribution of a revolving palisade to the Other World.[2]

---

motive appearing in Loeg's protection by Liban in the *Serglige*. The kind words of praise addressed by Bláthnat to Cuchulinn in the *Fled Bricrend*, after he has leaped into the revolving castle of her husband, should be remembered. In a modern tale, *The Bare Stripping Hangman* (*Waifs and Strays of Celtic Tradition*, III, 96–97), the hero, in distress at the castle of a giant, is rescued by the sister of the heroine, who takes him into the castle through an iron door in the wall and heals his wounds. (It will be remembered that Liban is sister to Fand.)

[1] The incident of reaching a land beneath the waves is common enough (see, for example, a tale of modern Brittany, *Rev. Celt.*, II, 308). An instance not before compared is in the *Romance of Reinbroun* (preserved in the Auchinleck MS., which dates from 1327), ed. Zupitza, E.E.T.S., sts. 80 ff. Reinbroun rides through a gate into a hill. The gate is shut and he rides half a mile in darkness. He comes to a palace surrounded by a broad water. He plunges, horse and all, into the water and goes to the bottom, thirty yards over helm, but reaches the palace at last. No one grows old there.

[2] Of course this does not prove that the incident was an invention of the Celts. Compare Hugo's palace at Constantinople, which, according to the *Journey of Charlemagne*, revolved on its axis by the operation of the wind (Child, *Ballads*, I, 276). Cf. also Chaucer, *Hous of Fame*, iii, 1918 ff., where the house of Dædalus is said to revolve.

There is a Welsh poem in the *Book of Taliessin*[1] called *The Victims of the Other World* which gives us reason to believe that this conception of a revolving barrier or a dangerous gateway at the entrance of the Other World was well known to the Welsh also. This poem, which is expressed in the obscure language of the early bards, tells of a voyage made by Arthur to Annwn for the purpose of rescuing the captive Gwair.[2] Like the Irish Other World, Annwn is regarded as an island lying beyond the sea:

PREIDDEN ANNWN.[3]

I.

I will praise the sovereign, supreme king of the land,
Who hath extended his dominion over the shore of the world.
Complete was the prison of Gweir [4] in Caer Sidi,[5]
Through the spite of Pwyll and Pryderi.
No one before him went into it.
The heavy blue chain held the faithful youth,
And before the spoils of Annwvn woefully he sings,
And till doom shall continue a bard of prayer.
Thrice enough to fill Prydwen we went into it;
Except seven none returned from Caer Sidi.

---

[1] This MS. dates from the early part of the fourteenth century (Skene, *Four Books*, I, 3). As the poem bears no traces of the influence of French romance, it is fair to infer that it is based on early Welsh conceptions.

[2] This explanation is given by Stephens, *Literature of the Kymry*, p. 273, where also a text and a translation of the poem may be found (pp. 183–190). I have followed the later and more accurate translation in Skene.

[3] Quoted from Skene, *Four Books*, I, 264–266; for the text, see II, 181–182.

[4] There is a triad (*Myv. Arch.*, p. 80, l. 30, quoted by Stephens, *Lit. of the Kymry*, p. 190) that mentions the captivity of the family of Gair ap Geirion, lord of Geirionydd, as one of the three closest ever known.

[5] Caer Sidi is mentioned also in another poem of the *Book of Taliessin* (No. xiv), part of which runs thus (Taliessin is the speaker):

> Complete is my chair in Caer Sidi,
> No one will be afflicted with disease or old age that may be in it.
> It is known to Manawd and Pryderi.
> Three utterances, around the fire, will he sing before it,
> And around its borders are the streams of Ocean,
> And the fruitful fountain is above it,
> Is sweeter than white wine the liquor therein (Skene, I, 276; text, II, 154).

II.

Am I not a candidate for fame, if a song is heard?
In Caer Pedryvan,[1] four its revolutions;
In the first word from the cauldron when spoken,
From the breath of nine maidens it was gently warmed.
Is it not the cauldron of the chief of Annwvn? What is its intention?
A ridge about its edge of pearls.
It will not boil the food of a coward, that has not been sworn,
A sword bright gleaming to him was raised,
And in the hand of Lleminawg it was left
And before the door of the gate of Uffern [2] the lamp was burning.
And when we went with Arthur, a splendid labour,
Except seven, none returned from Caer Vedwyd.[3]

III.

Am I not a candidate for fame with the listened song?
In Caer Pedryvan, *in the isle of the strong door ?*
The twilight and pitchy darkness were mixed together.
Bright wine their liquor before their retinue.
Thrice enough to fill Prydwen we went on the sea,
Except seven none returned from Caer Rigor.[4]

IV.

I shall not deserve much from the ruler of literature,
Beyond Caer Wydyr they saw not the prowess of Arthur.
Three score Canhwr stood on the wall,
Difficult was a conversation with its sentinel.

From a comparison of these lines it will be seen that Caer Sidi is a Land of Youth surrounded by the sea. It is connected with the Other-World power Manawyddan (= Manawd), and with Pwyll and Pryderi. This is consistent with the Mabinogi, *Pwyll Prince of Dyvet,* which calls Pwyll "Prince of Annwn." Pryderi is his son and successor. Rhŷs, *Arthurian Legend,* p. 301, connects Sidi with the Welsh *sidyll,* "a spinning wheel," and translates *Caer Sidi* by "revolving castle."

[1] "The quadrangular enclosure": Stephens.

[2] "Hell": Stephens.

[3] "The enclosure of the perfect ones": Stephens.   "The Castle of Revelry": Rhŷs, *Arthurian Legend,* p. 301.

[4] "The enclosure of the royal party": Stephens.

Thrice enough to fill Prydwen[1] there went with Arthur,
Except seven none returned from Caer Golud.

Although in this poem Annwn is once called *Uffern* ("hell"), yet it has in the main the well-known characteristics of the Celtic Happy Other World. It contains a magic cauldron that presumably furnishes inexhaustible food, and the inhabitants are described as "drinking the bright wine." It is also called "The Enclosure of the Perfect Ones." That it can be entered by a difficult gateway only, is evident. It is called "The Island of the Strong Door" and is said to be "four times revolving."

It is perfectly clear, then, that a revolving barrier, or an active door of some kind,[2] was a widespread motive of Celtic Other-World

---

[1] The text of this refrain runs: "Tri lloneit prytwen yd aeth gan arthur." I venture to suggest that this peculiar expression refers to a magic quality of the ship Prytwenn, by virtue of which it could contain any number, however great. It is the ship in which Arthur journeys to the Other World. It is usual in Celtic tales for the ship that takes the hero to the Land beyond the Waves to be the gift of a *fée,* and of a marvellous character, often having the property of folding up or expanding. See *Harvard Studies and Notes,* VII, 199, note 1, where I have cited many references to boats of this sort. A typical example is in Curtin, *Hero-Tales of Ireland,* p. 249, where a staff thrown into the sea becomes a ship. It can be "put back into a staff again" and borne in the hand. It will be remembered that Arthur was finally carried off to Avalon in a mysterious ship. Prytwenn is probably the same sort of ship as the boat of glass that carried off Connla, which apparently could accomplish any distance before night, and as the bronze boat that ferried Loeg over to Labraid's isle. Doubtless, like Arthur's sword Caliburnus (Geoffrey, *Historia,* IX, 4), it was brought from Avalon. Layamon (vv. 22,736 ff.) ascribes to Arthur a magical table; Geoffrey, l.c., ascribes to him not only the sword Caliburnus, but a marvellous lance *Ron* and a shield *Priwen;* while in *Kulhwch and Olwen* (Rhŷs and Evans, *Red Book of Hergest,* I, 105) there is a considerable list of belongings, including Prytwenn, ascribed to Arthur. These objects all have names and are treated as very valuable. They are probably all magical. This at least is the conclusion to which analogy leads. See the list of magical things given by Manannán to Lugh (above, p. 42, note), among ·which is a sword very much resembling Caliburnus. There is no ship in the list, but there is a horse that travels equally well by land and sea. Doubtless he fills the place of a ship as a means of reaching the Other World.

[2] In Laistner, *Das Rätsel der Sphinx,* Berlin, 1889, I, 263, there is mentioned, as an obstacle on the way to the Other World, a door that ever slams to and fro. This reference I owe to Professor Kittredge.

story. *A priori*, therefore, we have reason to believe that it must have been present in the material that Chrétien used when he was writing his *Ivain*. What could he do with the motive, supposing he decided to keep it at all? Would he not naturally rationalize it into the familiar portcullis, to be seen at every castle gate? This I believe to have been the origin of the sharp iron portcullis in the *Ivain*, that descended, "aussi con deables d'anfer" (v. 944), behind the hero and cut his steed in two.[1] In view of the numerous

---

[1] An interesting parallel that should be quoted at this point, because it appears to show this motive at an intermediate stage of development, is the story of *La Mule sans Frein* (Méon, *Nouveau Recueil de Fabliaux*, I, 1 ff.). This is a French poem and was written about the year 1200, but its similarity to the kind of Other-World story that has been studied above is so great that its essential dependence on Celtic tradition can hardly be denied:

A damsel, riding a mule without a bridle, came to Arthur's court and asked for the help of a knight to recover her bridle for her. Kay set out first, and his unsuccessful attempt is contrasted with the victorious exploit of the hero Gawain, in the same way that the failures of Loegaire and Conall are set off against the success of Cuchulinn in the *Fled Bricrend*. Gawain rode over a bridge consisting of a single narrow iron bar which spanned a terrible river, and found a narrow path leading to a castle. A broad water encircled the castle. The walls were decked with the heads of former adventurers, set upon spikes, and but one spike was empty. The castle was always turning like a mill-wheel or a top. Gawain spurred the mule, and made a rush for the gate as it came round. The mule got through *with the loss of half her tail*. There was a *vilain* in the castle, black as a Moor, who played the beheading game with Gawain. When Gawain had come off successfully from this and other tests, he was entertained by a lady, sister to the Damsel of the Mule. She would fain have persuaded Gawain to remain with her and be her lord and lord of all her castles. But Gawain refused, took the bridle, and departed.

If the revolving-castle motive, which we know to have been a part of Celtic stories of the Journey to the Other World, had reached a form like this before it came to the hands of Chrétien, how easy it would have been for him to change the cutting in two of the mule's tail into the more thrilling incident of the horse and the portcullis!

The resemblance between *La Mule sans Frein* and the *Fled Bricrend* is obvious. In both there is a turning castle, and in both an ugly black giant who proposes the head-cutting game. When the heroes first visited Curoi in the *Fled Bricrend*, it will be remembered that they fell into a magic mist that caused them to lose their way. A parallel to this incident occurs in a turning-castle episode in *Wigalois* (ed. Pfeiffer, Leipzig, 1847, cols. 173–181, vv. 6714–7053). The hero, in

parallels to this development in modern Celtic stories quoted in the notes, this view appears highly probable, if not quite certain.

---

overcoming the enchanter Rôaz (a parallel figure to Curoi), was obliged to pass through a treacherous magic mist. He then came to a marble gate, before which ran a water-wheel upon an iron track:

> Des ein rat von êre pflac:
> daz lief umbe vor dem tor
> ûf îsenînen siulen enbor.
> ez treip ein wazzer daz was grôz:
> durch daz fûle mos ez flôz (vv. 6775 ff.).

The wheel was set with sharp swords and clubs. Wigalois at last entered the tower and was obliged to fight with a monster, half man, half horse, called " Marrîen," before the fiercer conflict against Rôaz took place. On a pillar before the castle gate was a marvellous shining gem. There is a revolving castle which Gawain enters on horseback in *Diu Krône*, by Heinrich von dem Türlîn (ed. Scholl, vv. 12,951 ff.), and also a giant who changes semblance in an extraordinary manner.

Revolving castles are rather common in modern Celtic Other-World tales. The modern tale of *Cucúlin* has been already cited (Curtin, *Myths and Folk-Lore of Ireland*, pp. 304–326). The tale of *Young Conall* is an interesting parallel (Curtin, *Hero-Tales of Ireland*, pp. 58–92, from County Kerry). When Conall arrived at the castle of the Yellow King, he saw three poles, of which two bore a skull apiece: "These are the heads of two kings' sons who came to win the Yellow King's daughter." Thought he, " I suppose mine will be the third." However, after a furious battle, Conall cut off the head of the Yellow King and married the daughter. He presently disregarded his mistress's injunction not to sleep in the open, and was punished by losing her. His adventures in recovering her were many, but she was at last found in a revolving prison-guarded castle. Similar tales containing the turning-castle incident are: *Blaiman, Son of Apple* (Curtin, *Hero-Tales*, pp. 373–406, from County Kerry), and *Coldfeet and the Queen of Lonesome Island* (Curtin, pp. 242–261, from County Kerry).

There are also a number of modern Other-World tales which contain variants of what may be called the active-door type. In the tale of *Morraha* (Larminie, *West Irish Folk-Tales*, pp. 10–30, from County Mayo), the hero set out in quest of the Sword of Light. His steed cleared three miles of fire at one leap, three miles of mountain at the next, and three miles of sea at the third. Morraha was well entertained by the young king and queen of the country in which he now found himself, and they directed him how to proceed. He took the best horse in the stable and went to the door of the giant Blue Niall. After having turned his horse's back to the door, he knocked and demanded the Sword of Light, at the same time putting spurs to his horse. But Blue Niall overtook him and, "as he was passing the gate, cut his horse in two." The next day Morraha

CHAPTER IV (*Continued*).

ANCIENT CELTIC STORIES OF THE JOURNEY TO THE
OTHER WORLD.

VI. THE OTHER-WORLD LANDSCAPE.

THE extraordinary features of the landscape at the Fountain Perilous in the *Ivain* may be briefly recalled : The fountain, which
boils like hot water, though it is in fact colder than marble, is shaded
by the most beautiful tree in the world. This tree never loses its

---

had the same adventure, except that "as he was passing the gate" Blue Niall
"cut the horse in two and half the saddle with him." On the third day, "as he
was passing the gate," the giant "cut away the saddle and the clothes from his
back." Morraha at last went at night and overcame the giant.

In the tale of *Art and Balor Beimenach* (Curtin, *Hero-Tales*, pp. 327 ff., from
County Kerry), the hero has a similar adventure, thrice repeated ; only in this
case the giant cuts the horse in two as he is leaping the wall of the castle. "Art
tumbled down from the wall with his life."

Another Irish tale containing the incident of the severed horse at a giant's
castle, is printed by O'Foharta, *Zt. f. celt. Phil.*, I, 477 ff. In none of these tales,
we should observe, is it said that the horse is cut in two *by* the gate, but only *at*
the gate. However, the resemblance to the incident of the Falling Gates in the
Ivain is certainly close. I suppose no one will maintain that these modern tales
are a degradation of the *Ivain*. They certainly seem to corroborate the conclusion drawn from *La Mule sans Frein*, that the theme of a horse severed at
the gate of the Other World, with great peril to the rider, may have been a part
of Celtic story before the time of Chrétien.

There are at least two modern Irish tales that represent the perilous gate to
the Other World as more or less in the form of a portcullis. In the story called
King's Son and White Bearded Scolog (Curtin, *Hero-Tales* pp. 168–172, from
Connemara), the gate of the giant's castle has "a pavement of sharp razors,
edges upward." "Long needles set as thickly as bristles in a brush were fixed
points downward under the lintel of the door and the door was low." The hero
was obliged to make his horse leap into the castle over the razors and under the
needles. Practically the same sort of gate to a giant's castle appears in *The
King of Erin and the Queen of Lonesome Island* (Curtin, *Myths and Folk-Lore*,
pp. 93–113).

There is a curious tale obtained by David Fitzgerald at Askeaton in Ireland in
1879 (*Rev. Celt.*, IV, 185–186). Lake Guirr, "all Munster knows, is enchanted ; but

leaves, winter or summer. It is a pine, and the tallest[1] that ever grew on earth. Its foliage must be very thick, for, however hard it rains, not a drop can pass its branches. Singing birds gather so thickly on this tree that they entirely conceal its branches and its leaves. Though each bird sings a different note, their voices together make the most delightful harmony imaginable. No one will ever hear aught so beautiful unless he go thither to listen to them.

To sum up the chief features of the description, there is (1) a magnificent tree, (2) whose leaves do not fade summer or winter, and

---

the spell passes off it once in every seven years. The lake then, to whoever has the luck to behold it, appears dry; and the Tree may be partly seen at the bottom of it, covered with a Green Cloth. A certain bold fellow was at the spot one day at the very instant when the spell broke, and he rode his horse towards the tree and snatched away the Green Cloth (*Brat 'Uaine*) that covered it. As he turned his horse and fled for his life the Woman who sat on the watch, knitting under the cloth, at the foot of the tree, called out:

> Awake, awake, thou silent tide!
> From the Dead Women's Land a horseman rides,
> From my head the green cloth snatching.

At the words the waters rose; and so fiercely did they pursue him that as he gained the edge of the lake *one half of his steed* was swept away, and with it the [Green Cloth], which he was drawing after him. Had that been taken, the enchantment was ended for ever."

I have quoted the story in full to show the confused form in which Fitzgerald obtained it. Apparently it must have been originally a fairy mistress tale. The tree would then be a part of the Other-World landscape, and the incident of the halving of the steed a survival of some active-door episode. Fitzgerald gives also a well-defined fairy mistress tale connected with this lake.

It is curious to remember that "the fountain such that if touched, or even seen by a man, it forthwith deluged the whole province" described by Giraldus Cambrensis (1146–1220) in his *Top. Hib.* (dist. ii, cap. 7, Rolls ed., V, 89), was in this same province, Munster. The fountain (*fons*), says Giraldus, would not stop deluging the province till a priest celebrated mass in an adjoining chapel.

The only inference I wish to draw from these modern tales is that the Strong Door attributed to the Other World in ancient Celtic story becomes naturally rationalized into a falling portcullis, while the incident of a horse being cut in two at this gate is a common embellishment.

[1] This translation is based on a variant ascribed by Foerster to MS. G. The reading that he adopts in his text (v. 414) is not "the tallest" but a repetition of what was said before, "the most beautiful."

(3) whose foliage is so dense that rain cannot pass through it, (4) standing by a fountain. (5) The tree is full of birds, who sing not in unison, but in harmony, and (6) their song is really a divine service.[1]

This romantic landscape shows no signs of being a chance embellishment. It is described repeatedly, and one of Iwain's chief hopes, as he sets out on his journey, is that he may see the pine that overshadows the fountain. There is nothing, therefore, against an hypothesis that would explain this scene as a rationalization of an earlier Other-World landscape. On the contrary, no other adequate explanation has ever been suggested. With these facts in mind, we may turn to the study of the Other-World landscape in Celtic story.

In the *Serglige Conculaind*, which is the oldest extant tale of the precise type now under discussion, and which we have therefore used as a norm for comparison, the landscape of the Other World is rather fully described. It is marked by splendid trees full of singing birds. These trees bear fruit, and three hundred men are nourished by the fruit of each tree. One notable tree stands at the door of the Other-World palace, and the harmonious song of the birds upon it is particularly dwelt on. There is a noble well close at hand.

In the *Imram Brain*, the great antiquity of which seems certain, the same general features are described. One "ancient tree" is mentioned "from which birds call at the canonical hours" (§§ 6, 7).[2]

---

[1] S'escoutai tant qu'il orent fet
Lor servise trestot a tret (vv. 471–472).

[2] This singing to the Hours is obviously a borrowing from Christian conceptions of the Earthly Paradise. The birds are probably thought of as transformed souls (see *Mailduin*, § 19), awaiting the Day of Judgment, who chant the divine services at their appointed times. The fact that the influence of the Earthly Paradise has been at work at one point in this description naturally suggests that perhaps the notable tree may be a borrowing of the Christian Tree of Life (observe that its fruit feeds the Other-World people). At the same time, it must be remembered that the *Serglige* description (which bears no distinct marks of Christian influence), though it speaks of many trees, singles out one as of special prominence. A single tree with singing birds may well have been a part of pagan Celtic Other-World lore. The occurrence of an Other-World tree, perhaps due to Christian influence, in a document as ancient as the *Imram Brain*, has an important bearing on the vexed question of the origin of the ash Yggdrasill and the Scandinavian Other-World landscape in general. Christian influence may have operated *through* Ireland.

In another stanza (§ 43) " a wood without decay and without defect "
is spoken of. This reminds one of the tree in the *Ivain*, whose
leaves did not fade winter or summer.

The Celtic Other-World landscape, indeed, so far as it can be
recovered from these two extremely early tales, closely resembles
the scenery at the Fountain Perilous in the *Ivain*. In both there is
(1) a remarkable tree, (2) whose leaves do not decay, (4) standing
near a well, and (5) filled with singing birds, (6) who are performing a religious service. It will be observed that, except for the
single feature (3) of the tree's having branches so thick that no rain
could penetrate them, the list of important marks of the description
in the *Ivain* would apply equally well to that of the Other-World
landscape in these Irish tales. Even, therefore, if we were unable
to trace this motive any farther, the probability that the scene in the
Ivain is at bottom a rationalization of a Celtic Other-World landscape would be very great.

On the basis thus given, as has been said, it is entirely justifiable
to assume that the birds singing psalms on Island 18 of the *Mailduin*, the souls in bird shape on the trees of Island 19, and the marvellous fountain of Island 20 must originally have been united in
one landscape. A comparison of the later *imrama* establishes the
truth of this inference beyond the possibility of doubt.

In the *Imram Snedgusa ocus Mic Riagla*, which is preserved in a
fourteenth-century MS.,[1] but which has been shown by Zimmer[2]
to have originated about the end of the ninth century or during the
tenth, one of the adventures is as follows[3] :

Thereafter the wind wafts them to an island wherein was a great tree
with beautiful birds on its branches. [Here follows a distinctly ecclesias-
tical account of " a great bird with head of gold and wings of silver " that
told them tales out of the life of Christ (§ 17). The next section resumes :]

---

[1] *The Yellow Book of Lecan* (H. 2. 16. T. C. D.).

[2] *Haupt's Zt.*, XXXIII, 218 ff.

[3] Quoted from the translation of Whitley Stokes, published, with the Irish
text, in *Revue Celtique*, IX, 14–25. A summary of this tale is given by Zimmer,
l.c., pp. 211–216.

" Melodious was the music of those birds a-singing psalms and canticles praising the Lord. For they were the birds of the Plain of Heaven and neither trunk nor leaf of that tree decays " (§ 18).

In this passage occur, *united,* features 1, 2, 5, and 6 of the description in the *Ivain.* Moreover, between the phrase last quoted and a part of the account of the tree in the *Ivain* there is an almost verbal resemblance [1]:

SNEDGUS, § 18.	YVAIN, vv. 384–385.
And neither trunk nor leaf of that tree decays.	An toz tans la fuelle li dure, Qu'il ne la pert por nul iver.

In the Latin *Navigatio Sancti Brandani,* — which, as Zimmer has shown,[2] is based in great part on the Irish *imrama* (especially the *Imram Mailduin*), and is preserved in several MSS. considerably older than the time of Chrétien, — occur the fountain, the tree, and the birds united in a single landscape, forming a parallel to the *Ivain* that, as Kölbing has remarked, cannot be purely accidental.

In the *Navigatio* [3] the voyagers arrive at an island which, as they have been previously informed,[4] is called *Paradysus Avium.* They find the mouth of a river, and with the aid of a rope they tow their boat up the

---

[1] This and several other parallels discussed in the next few pages were pointed out by the late Professor Kölbing in an article entitled *Christian von Troyes Yvain und die Brandanuslegende,* in *Zt. f. vergleich. Litteraturgeschichte,* XI, 442–448. Kölbing justly felt that these coincidences could not be due to chance, but it did not occur to him that they proved a definite connection between the whole story of the *Ivain* and the *imrama.* He feels obliged to admit that Chrétien, in his description of the landscape at the Fountain Perilous, must have borrowed from various pieces of *imram* literature (he did not trace the theme back to fairy mistress stories like the *Serglige*) ; but he does not attempt to explain why Chrétien should have copied this material into his narrative. It is useless to the action and is scarcely the sort of ornament that a rationalizer like Chrétien would have gone out of his way to adopt. Why should it appear in the *Ivain* unless it was thrust upon him by the original story ?

[2] *Haupt's Zt.,* XXXIII, 298. Zimmer dated the *Navigatio* not earlier than 1050; but Steinweg, *Rom. Forsch.,* VII, 1–48, cites a MS. of about 1000. Kölbing, l.c., p. 443, gives as date "the second half of the twelfth century."

[3] *Sanct Brandan,* ed. C. Schröder, p. 11, ll. 19 ff.

[4] P. 10, l. 18.

stream "dum ad fontem venerant ejusdem fluminis. . . . Erat autem super illo [sc. fonte] arbor mire latitudinis in gyrum et non magne altitudinis, cooperta avibus candidissimis: in tantum cooperuerunt illam, ut folia et rami ejus vix viderentur."

One of these birds addresses Brandan and tells him that they are really spirits in bird shape.[1] "Hic presentiam Dei non possumus videre, set in tantum alienavit nos a consortio aliorum qui steterunt, quia vagamur per diversas partes aeris et firmamenti et terrarum sicut alii spiritus qui mittuntur, sed in sanctis diebus atque dominicis accipimus corpora talia qualia tu nunc vides, ut commoremur hic laudemusque nostrum creatorem." . . . It is added[2]: "Cum autem vespertina hora appropinquasset, ceperunt omnes aves qui in arbore erant quasi una voce cantare percutientes latera sua atque dicentes: 'Te decet ymnus, Deus in Syon, et tibi reddetur votum in Jherusalem.' Et semper reciprocabant predictum versiculum quasi per spacium unius hore, et videbatur viro Dei et illis qui cum eo erant illa modulatio ex sonis alarum quasi carmen planctus pro suavitate."

Thus the birds sang at the various canonical hours: "ad terciam vigiliam noctis," "ad vesperum," "cum aurora refulsisset," "ad nonam." "Ita die ac nocte aves reddebant Deo laudem."

There are, as Kölbing has indicated, two remarkable verbal resemblances between this description in the *Navigatio* and that in the *Ivain*:

NAVIGATIO, pp. 11, l. 31 ; 12, ll. 26 ff.　　　YVAIN, vv. 462, 465 ff.

Ut folia et rami ejus vix viderentur.　　Qu'il n'i paroit branche ne fuelle.

. . . . . .　　　　　　　. . . . . .

Ceperunt omnes aves que in arbore　Et trestuit li oisel chantoient,
　erant, quasi una voce cantare.　　Si que trestuit s'antracordoient.

It is, moreover, clear that in both cases the birds are engaged in a religious service, for this must be the meaning of the expression in the *Ivain*:

　　　S'escoutai tant qu'il orent fet
　　　Lor servise trestot a tret (vv. 471–472).[3]

---

[1] P. 12, ll. 16 ff.　　　　　　[2] P. 12, ll. 26 ff.

[3] Chrétien's words might possibly mean "until they had finished their office or duty"; but Kölbing points out that the phrase "feire servise" is regularly applied to a religious office, and compares the corresponding passage in the *Ivens Saga*, ii, 37: "þar .til er þeir luku søng sínum ok tíðum [the canonical hours] er þeir sungu." Cf. Kölbing, *Ivens Saga*, Halle, 1898, pp. 16–17, footnote.

There is an Anglo-Norman version of the Brandan story which was composed by Benedeit about the year 1121. The corresponding incident in this is also strikingly like the description in the *Ivain.* The most important of these resemblances, which are occasionally even verbal, may be conveniently indicated by an arrangement in parallel columns:

BRANDAN,[1] vv. 489 ff.

Al chef del duit out une arbre
Itant blanche cume marbre
E les fuiles mult sunt ledes
De ruge blanc taceledes
De haltece par vedue
Muntout le arbre sur la nue
Des le sumet desque en terre
La brancheie mult la serre
E ledement s'estent par l'air
Umbraiet luin e tolt l'eclair
Tute asise de blancs oiseus
Unches nul hom ne vit tant beus.

YVAIN, vv. 380 ff.

La fontainne verras, qui bout,
S'est ele plus froide que marbres.
Onbre li fet li plus biaus arbres
Qu'onques poïst feire nature.
An toz tans la fuelle li dure,
Qu'il ne la pert por nul iver.

YVAIN, vv. 413 ff.

Bien sai de l'arbre, c'est la fins,
Que ce estoit li plus biaus pins
Qui onques sor terre creüst.
Ne cuit qu'onques si fort pleüst
Que d'iaue i passast une gote,
Einçois coloit par desus tote.

YVAIN, vv. 459 ff.

Des que li tans fu trespassez,
Vi sor le pin tant amassez
Oisiaus (s'est qui croire m'an vuelle),
Qu'il n'i paroit branche ne fuelle,
Que tot ne fust covert d'oisiaus,
S'an estoit li arbres plus biaus ;
Et trestuit li oisel chantoient
Si que trestuit s'antracordoient :
Mes divers chanz chantoit chascuns.

---

[1] Quoted from Suchier's text, *Rom. Stud.*, I, 553–588. For convenience, abbreviations are here resolved and words are separated, but no punctuation has been attempted. Cf. Auracher's text, vv. 438 ff., *Zt. f. rom. Phil.*, II, 444 ff. On the date of Benedeit's *Brandan* (about 1121), see Suchier, p. 553. With this date Kölbing (l.c., p. 444) agrees and also G. Paris (*Rom.*, XXIX, 590, n.te 1).

All of the chief features of the landscape at the Fountain Perilous are to be found in this Anglo-Norman *Voyage of Brandan*, including even the dense foliage of the tree,[1] so that the summary which I have given of the features of the incident in the *Ivain* would apply equally well to the Anglo-Norman poem. In comparing the two narratives, Kölbing has directed attention to the identical rhyme-words [2] occurring at about the same point in the two episodes; also to the fact that in both the tree is described as especially adapted by the form of its branches for casting a shadow,[3] and to the extraordinary height of the tree in the *Brandan :*

> De haltece par vedue
> Muntout le arbre sur la nue (vv. 493–494),

which is paralleled in the reading of one of the manuscripts [4] of the *Ivain :*

> Que ce estoit li plus hauz pins
> Qui onques sor terre creüst (vv. 414–415),

and in the corresponding verse in Hartmann's *Iwein :*

> Si ist breit *hôch* und alsô dic
> daz regen noch der sunnen blic
> niemer dar durch kumt (vv. 575 ff.).

From a comparison of these voyage-stories with the description of the scenery at the Fountain Perilous, Kölbing has come to the conclusion that Chrétien must have borrowed " dieses ganze Motiv von dem mit Vögeln dicht besetzten Baume " from the Brandan legend. He thinks the French poet must have had at hand the *Navigatio*, and probably also the Norman-French *Brandan*, and that he certainly must have known the incident in the *Imram Snedgus.*

---

[1] " La brancheie mult la serre " (v. 496).

[2] *Brandan*, vv. 489–490, *arbre, marbre ; Yvain*, vv. 381–382, *marbres, arbres.*

[3] *Brandan*, v. 498, "umbraie luin "; *Yvain*, v. 382, " Onbre li fet li plus biaus arbres."

[4] This reading is more attractive than that adopted in the text of Foerster's editions, "li plus biaus pins," which merely repeats v. 382: "li plus biaus arbres." Kölbing thinks it certain that some texts of the *Navigatio* must have made the tree *high* (the version that we have reads " non magne altitudinis "), for in a fragment of an Old Norse version of the Brandan story the tree is called "einkar hátt " (Unger, *Heilagra Manna Sögur*, I, 275).

A moment's reflection will show that this is a very difficult hypothesis to maintain. Why should Chrétien have pieced together his description from various stories? The situation is not what it would be if the landscape formed an important element in Chrétien's plot. In that case one might possibly argue that Chrétien had been at great pains to put together his description from various hints. As it is, the accessories of the fountain (the tree, the birds, etc.) being mere ornaments, tending rather to interrupt the progress of the story, such a useless activity on his part is almost unthinkable. A far more probable inference to draw from the fact that Chrétien seems at one point to agree with the description in one story, while at another point he agrees with that in another,[1] is that we have not the particular originals that Chrétien used, but only stories containing the same theme, — namely, descriptions of the conventional landscape of the Celtic Other World, which had become identified with that of the Earthly Paradise. This will explain the presence in the *Ivain* of numerous apparently petty and purely decorative details, without our assuming that Chrétien purposely gathered them together out of different voyage-stories.

Kölbing, who does not attempt to explain how this extraordinary landscape made its way into the *Ivain*, recognizes distinctly its Other-World character. He compares the monkish *Visio Tnugdali*, which was composed between 1150 and 1160.[2] When Tundalus reached Paradise he found a scene unmistakably the same as that which we have traced in the Celtic *imrama*, in the *Navigatio*, and in the *Ivain*:

Et respiciens vidit unam arborem maximam et latissimam, frondibus et floribus viridissimam omniumque frugum generibus fertilissimam. In cujus frondibus, aves multe diversorum colorum et diversarum vocum cantantes et organizantes morabantur, sub cujus etiam ramis lilia et rose multe nimis et cunctarum herbarum specierumque odiferarum genera oriebantur.

---

[1] Thus the *Ivain* agrees with the *Snedgus* in the unfading leaves ascribed to the tree (a feature not mentioned in the *Navigatio*), while it agrees with the *Navigatio* in the birds' gathering so thickly that they obscure the branches and the leaves (a feature not mentioned in the *Snedgus*).

[2] Ed. A. Wagner, p. 50. Wagner discusses the date of the *Visio* on page xxv.

The extraordinary size of the tree in this scene, the numerous birds, and especially their singing in harmony, form, taken together, a parallel that cannot be due to chance. This passage, and others that might be cited, prove that the scene whose development is now under discussion must have been well understood in Chrétien's time as the conventional landscape of the Other World or the Earthly Paradise. There is, therefore, no reasonable hypothesis that will account for Chrétien's insertion of this theme *ab extra* into his *Ivain.* There are many things that show that he minimized the marvellous character of the incidents he was relating. It would be absurd, then, to hold that he went out of his way to drag in the landscape of the Other World. Its occurrence in the *Ivain* must be a survival from that Celtic story of a journey to the Other World which, as the cumulative evidence of many other incidents tends to show, lay at the basis of the tale of Iwain.

Practically every Celtic tale of a fairy mistress contains a description of the Other-World landscape. We have studied such descriptions in the *Serglige,* the *Bran,* the *Mailduin,* the *Snedgus,* and the *Adventures of Teigue.* Similar descriptions are to be found in less ancient tales, such as the *Imram curraig Húi Corra,*[1] the *Baile an*

---

[1] *The Voyage of the Húi Corra* exists in the *Book of Fermoy,* a fifteenth-century MS. It has been edited and translated by Stokes, *Rev. Celt.,* XIV, 22–70. Stokes puts the composition of the tale in the eleventh century. Zimmer (*Haupt's Zt.,* XXXIII, 198) thinks it "not earlier than the twelfth century." A passage in the early part of this *imram* runs thus :

"Thereafter I perceived that I was borne away to gaze at Heaven, and I perceived the Lord himself on his throne, and a bird-flock of angels making music to him. Then I saw a bright bird and sweeter was his singing than every melody. Now this was Michael in the form of a bird in the presence of the Creator " (§ 14).

Later the voyagers come to what seems to be the Earthly Paradise :

"Thereafter they row on for a long while, till another wonderful island was shewn to them, with a beautiful bright grove of fragrant apple trees therein. A very beautiful river flowed through the midst of the grove. Now when the wind would move the tree tops of the grove, sweeter was their song than any music. The Húi Corra ate somewhat of the apples and drank somewhat of the river of wine, so that they were straightway satisfied, and perceived not wound or disease in them " (§ 47).

Sceal,[1] the *Echtra Cormaic*,[2] and many others.   If, then, the material
that Chrétien used in writing his *Ivain* was essentially a Celtic fairy
tale, he must almost certainly have found in it an account of the
Other-World landscape.   The occurrence, therefore, of unmistakable

---

[1] The *Baile na Scail* is an Other-World Journey found in a fourteenth-century MS.
It must, however, be at least as old as the eleventh century, for it was known to
Flann of Monasterboice, who died in 1056 (O'Curry, *MS. Materials*, pp. 387–389,
and Appendix, p. cxxviii).   In it the Other-World tree is particularly dwelt on:
" A kingly rath they saw with a beautiful tree at the door."

[2] The *Echtra Cormaic i Tir Tairngiri* exists in no MS. older than the fourteenth century.   The text, according to Zimmer (*Haupt's Zt.*, XXXIII, 268) is
at least somewhat older than that.   It has been edited and translated by Stokes,
Irische Texte, III, i, 183–212:

One day Cormac was alone in the plain near Tara when he saw a gray-haired
warrior coming to him.   He had in his hand a branch which when shaken put
every one who heard it to sleep by the melody which it made.   " Whence hast thou
come?" said Cormac.   "From a land," he replied, "where there is naught save
truth and where there is neither old age nor decay nor gloom."   Cormac asked
for the music-making branch and received it after promising to give the warrior in
return whatever three boons he should ask.

A year later the stranger reappeared and asked for Cormac's daughter, whom
he took away with him.   Again he came and took Cormac's son, and last of all
his wife.   Cormac endured this not, but followed after the stranger.   He soon
found himself alone on a plain with a wall of bronze around it.   " He sees in the
garth a shining fountain, with five streams flowing out of it, and the hosts in turn
a-drinking its water.   Nine hazels of Buan ... drop their nuts into the fountain. ...
Now the sound of the falling of those streams is more melodious than any music
that (men) sing."   Cormac entered the palace and found a noble warrior with the
loveliest of the world's women.   He was entertained and bathed without the aid
of any attendants.   " The (heated) stones (of themselves went) into and (came)
out (of the water)."

The warrior now brought forth Cormac's family and bestowed on him many
gifts, saying: "I am Manannán mac Lir.   To see the Land of Promise have I
brought thee hither."   After a banquet, all went to rest.   When Cormac awoke
in the morning, he found himself on the plain of Tara, and beside him were his
wife, his son, and his daughter, and also all the presents that Manannán had
given him.

It will be remembered that, when Teigue reached the Other World, he found
Connla established there as a prince, having beside him " the damsel of many
charms that brought him thither."   Now in the *Dinnshenchas of Sinend* in the
Book of Leinster (p. 156, a, 6) we read of an Other-World fountain called " Connla's
Well ":

traces of an Other-World landscape in the *Ivain* cannot but add much weight to the cumulative evidence of other incidents, which tends to show that the *Ivain* is at bottom a Celtic Other-World tale.

The Other-World landscape, as it appears in even the older Irish tales, is evidently in part, perhaps in very great part, a product of Christian influences. This fact in no way militates against the hypothesis that the episode reached Chrétien through Celtic channels.[1] The elements of the description, though perhaps in great

---

"Sinend, daughter of Lodan mac Lir, out of the Land of Promise, went to Connla's Well, which is under sea. That is the well at which are the hazels of wisdom, that is, the hazels of the science of poetry, and in the same hour their fruit, their blossom, and their foliage break forth." (See *Rev. Celt.*, XV, 457.)

Although this description may have been influenced by the classic fountain of the Muses, it certainly seems to show that, as early as 1150, a part of the Other-World landscape was definitely connected with Connla. Perhaps the *Echtra Condla* existed once in a more complete form, in which the Other-World landscape was described.

It will also be remembered that in the *Adventures of Teigue*, the hero, when he returns, is told that the Other World birds will go with him : "They will give you guidance and make you symphony and minstrelsy, and till again ye reach Ireland neither sadness or grief shall afflict you." These birds seem to be a part of the Other-World landscape, even if their guiding the hero suggests the possibility that classical influence has been at work in this passage. A guiding falcon is found in the *Mailduin*, § 34 (cf. *Æneid*, VI, 190 ff.). The birds of Riannon, the Other-World wife of Pwyll, should be compared at this point. In *Branwen, Daughter of Llyr* (Loth, *Les Mabinogion*, I, 91–93) Bran directs his followers to go to Harddlech, "where they will remain seven years at table while the birds of Rhiannon sing to them." They do as he tells them, and "three birds came and sang more beautifully than any birds they had ever heard. The birds kept far out over the sea, but they saw them as distinctly as if they were close at hand." This lasted for seven years.

The birds in the last two passages, though probably at bottom a part of the apparatus of the Celtic Other World, have perhaps been influenced a good deal by non-Celtic tradition. Professor Kittredge has called to my attention the birds to which the Monk Felix listened. Felix fell asleep at their music, and, when he awoke and returned to his monastery, he found that he had been absent two hundred years. For the text of this story and for references, see Waitz, *Göttinger Gesellschaft. d. Wiss., Hist.-phil. Classe, Abhandl.*, VIII, 7 ff.; cf. *Zt. f. d. Phil.*, XIV, 96; XXVIII, 35 ff.

[1] The same remark is to be made in general about the incidents discussed in this chapter. They have all been found as parts of Celtic fairy mistress story

part Christian, did not take their peculiar development except on Celtic ground.   It is only on Celtic ground that stories written before the time of Chrétien can be pointed out that contain all of the important features of the landscape at the Fountain Perilous.

Few things are, therefore, more certain than that the marvellous landscape of Chrétien's Fountain is derived from Celtic sources. The long line of parallels to this incident, running back at least to the eighth century, is enough to establish this beyond a reasonable doubt.

CHAPTER IV (*Concluded*).

ANCIENT CELTIC STORIES OF THE JOURNEY TO THE OTHER WORLD.

VII. CONCLUSION.

THE result of the investigations in this chapter seems to be the complete establishment of all the parallels between the *Ivain* and the *Serglige* tentatively put forth on p. 44 above.   The Marvellous Landscape at the Fountain Perilous has been shown to be the same as that in Labraid's isle.   The Combat Motive in the *Ivain* has been exactly paralleled in an ancient Irish tale of the type of the *Serglige*.   The Falling Gates have been traced by natural transitions to the Perilous-Passage Motive.   The other parallels between the *Ivain* and the *Serglige* — the tale of a previous adventurer, the part played by the heroine's *confidante*, the departure of the hero to his own land, his broken faith, followed by his loss of the heroine and his madness — need no study to confirm their significance.

---

before the time of Chrétien. This is all that it is necessary to prove for our present purpose.   That some of them are perhaps not of Celtic invention, but may have been early Celtic borrowings from what one writer has called " the common stock of European folk-lore," is of no consequence in the present argument, which is concerned with the question of Chrétien's immediate sources.

These coincidences between Chrétien's *Ivain* and a single particular type of ancient Irish and Welsh story cannot reasonably be regarded as due to chance. The *Ivain* must in origin be a Celtic story of a Journey to the Other World, of the type conveniently represented by the *Serglige Conculaind*.

CHAPTER V.

LATER CELTIC STORIES OF THE JOURNEY TO THE OTHER WORLD.

IN the great collection of tales called *The Colloquy with the Men of Old* (*Acallamh na Senórach*), preserved in manuscripts of the fifteenth century,[1] there is a story of the Journey to the Other World which illustrates very well the partial rationalization which the older themes generally undergo when they pass through the hands of later redactors. In this tale the Other-World heroine is represented as the daughter of the arch-ollave of Manannán mac Lir, and the hero is said to have eloped with her. These rather stupid attempts at rationalization[2] do not, however, prevent the original fairy character of the lady from coming out distinctly. Though the story in the *Acallamh* is only an episode, it will be convenient to give it a title from the name of the hero:

---

[1] The fragments occurring in the *Book of Lismore* (including this tale) are printed by O'Grady, *Silva Gadelica*, I, 94–234 (translation, II, 101–265). The whole *Acallamh* has since been edited, from four MSS., by Stokes, *Irische Texte*, IV, i, 1–438, with a translation of such passages as are not found in the *Book of Lismore*. The story which here concerns us is considerably older than the fifteenth century.

[2] The fact that the tale has suffered rationalization goes to show that its original form must be old.

THE STORY OF CIABÁN.[1]

Ciabán put to sea with two strangers in a boat. Caught in a dreadful storm, the voyagers were like to perish when they saw a horseman on a dark green steed with a golden bridle, riding over the waves. He took the three travellers up on the back of his horse, while the boat floated along beside, and in this way they came to the Land of Promise (*Tír Thairrn-gaire*). There they dismounted and went to Manannán's *cathair* (stone fort), " in which an end had just been made of ordering a banqueting hall for them." [2] " All four were served there : their horns and their cups were raised : comely dark-eyed gillies went round with smooth polished horns : sweet-stringed timpans were played by them and most melodious dulcet-chorded harps, until the whole house was flooded with music." " Now in the Land of Promise, Manannán possessed an arch-ollave that had three daughters. The three travellers eloped with these three daughters." Ciabán carried off the one named Clidna and reached Ireland with her.

Although in this tale the fairy character of the lady has been lost sight of, yet in some verses that are sung she is called "the queen of the distant gathering," an apparent survival of her primitive exalted position. The incident of meeting Manannán on the sea is found in the oldest tales. In the *Serglige* and the *Bran*, however, Manannán drives a chariot. Horseback riding is probably a later feature, though not necessarily very late. Loegaire, according to the *Book of Leinster*, returned from the Other World on horseback. In Celtic story the Other World is reached either in a marvellous ship, which is presumably the earlier motive, or by means of a horse that travels on the sea as well as on the land.[3] The tale of Ciabán is interesting as showing one motive as it were in process of transformation into the other. The travellers start in a boat,[4] but finish their journey on the back of a horse.

---

[1] Summarized from O'Grady, *Silva Gadelica*, II, 198–201. For text, see Stokes, *Irische Texte*, IV, i, 106 ff.

[2] I.e. the coming of the travellers is expected, as is always the case in the Other World.

[3] For example, in the *Fate of the Children of Tuirean*, Lugh is said to have had Manannán's steed Enbarr, which travelled equally well by sea or by land.

[4] A marvellous self-moving boat as a means of communication with the Other World appears in the fairy mistress story of Becuma (summarized by Todd, from

There are numbers of later Irish Other-World stories belonging to the type exemplified in the older literature by the *Serglige*, the *Loegaire*, and the Welsh *Pwyll and Arawn*. In these stories, it will be remembered, the hero is in each case invited to the Other World by a fairy chieftain, who is oppressed by a mysterious enemy and needs the aid of a mortal hero to free him from his foe. As a reward, the hero in every case is promised and receives the hand of a *fée*.

The precise form in which the stories of this type have been handed down to us can only be explained, I think, by assuming that they have suffered more or less at the hands of rationalizers, who have modified the original relations of the supernatural actors to make them conform to ordinary human situations. All the Celtic fairy stories, with the exception of the *Echtra Condla*, show traces of having been influenced by a general tendency to represent the fairy folk as merely human beings living in a marvellous or distant land. Fairy relationships are interpreted after a strictly human pattern.[1] Liban, the messenger of Fand, is made the wife of Labraid, a king of the Other World. The *fée* in the tale of Loegaire is represented as the daughter of Fiachna, whom he bestows in marriage just as any earthly monarch would bestow his daughter. The Other World is often identified with the Isle of Man or the Hebrides or some other remote land. In the more modern stories this process has gone so far that the Other World is commonly represented as Greece, and the heroine, whose fairy character has been forgotten,

---

the *Book of Fermoy*, a fifteenth-century MS., *R.I.A.*, *Irish MS. Series*, I, 38 ff.). Manannán appears in this tale as a chieftain of the Tuatha de Danan. The tale of Finn and Bebend in the *Acallamh na Senórach* should also be compared (Stokes, *Irische Texte*, IV, i, 164 ff.; translation, O'Grady, *Silva Gadelica*, II, 238–242), where an Other-World personage escapes in a mysterious boat across the sea. Bebend (Bébind), a lady of supernatural beauty, visits Finn. She declares that she has come from the Land of Maidens across the Western Sea. She is the daughter of the king of that land, "who has nine daughters and one hundred and forty maidens." "There are no men there except the king and his three sons."

[1] It should be remembered that none of these story texts are much older, in their present form, than the tenth century. By that time the Irish had long been Christians, and doubtless already their conceptions of the fairies were becoming confused.

is called the daughter of the king of Athens. *Sorcha* [1] (Portugal) is another name applied to what must have been at first the Other World, while *Tír fá Thuinn* [2] is even explained as Holland.

If we make allowances for this progressive euhemerization, a more primitive form of the type of story now under discussion may be reconstructed as follows: The *fée* was probably always represented as supreme. She falls in love with a mortal and sends one of her maidens to invite him to her land. Several adventurers thereupon set out, but the *fée* appoints one of her creatures to guard the passage. Naturally, no one overcomes this opposing warrior but the destined hero, who is rewarded by the possession of the *fée*. But to the exalted character of the *fée* is joined a requirement of absolute obedience to her commands. Very often the hero offends in some way and is punished by instant dismissal. If he ever returns, it is only after many adventures.

If this be not the primitive form of the type of story with which we are dealing, how can one explain the fact that Labraid does not send some one of his officers to invite Cuchulinn to his land, espe cially after Cuchulinn has objected to going on the invitation of a woman? The coming of a woman, Liban, is an evident survival from an older form of the story, in which the *fée* and her maidens were the only real actors. Again, if this be not the original form of stories of this type, how can one explain the fact that Arawn offers his wife to Pwyll? "I will give thee the most beautiful woman thou hast ever seen to sleep with thee every night." This is a natural development if Arawn was at first only the creature of the *fée*, employed by her to lure the mortal on whom she had set her fancy to the Other World. The ruthless way, in the *Tale of Curoi*, in which Bláthnat marries Cuchulinn after the death of her husband, may also be taken as an indication that the giant was originally only a creature of the *fée*.

Of course, neither in the *Tale of Curoi* nor in any of the other tales just mentioned could the opposing warrior, in the most primitive form of the story, have been really slain. He was an Other-

---

[1] See Douglas Hyde, *The Lad of the Ferule*, p. xiv, note.
[2] "The Land beneath the Waves." See Hyde, p. 23, note.

World being, like the *fée*, and like her essentially immortal. This is clearly indicated in the case of Curoi, who, as we know from the *Fled Bricrend*, was thrice beheaded, but each time returned the next day as strong as ever. All of these supernatural creatures of the *fée*, Manannán, Arawn, Curoi, are shape-shifters. The opposing warrior is only apparently slain by the hero, not really put out of the way. The combat was in origin only a test of valor. Its object was to give the hero a chance to prove that he was worthy of the love of a *fée*.

When, however, the fairy nature of the Other-World people became more and more forgotten, the combat was regarded as a battle in earnest to get rid of a powerful opponent. The female *fées* were shorn of their absolute power, and men were introduced to play the leading parts, as on earth. Hence would naturally arise a situation like that in the *Serglige*, where the Other-World king is represented as oppressed by a foe and as sending for Cuchulinn to help him. The reward he promises is the hand of a *fée*, who is more or less rationalized and is represented as his sister-in-law. A slightly different turn in the rationalization would give the situation in the *Loegaire*, where the fairy king presents his daughter to the mortal hero who comes to his aid. Another and very natural turn would represent the Other-World power employed by the *fée* to test the hero's valor, as her husband.[1] This would give the situation in *Pwyll and Arawn*, in the *Tale of Curoi*, and, I may add, in the story of Laudine and Esclados.[2]

---

[1] The creature of the *fée* may have been thought of in the earliest times as her paramour, not of course as her husband in any strict sense, for the conventional relations of human marriage would not have been strictly applied to distinctly supernatural beings such as the primitive fairies undoubtedly were. Even if this supernatural being, really a god, were her paramour, she might have tired of him, as is hinted in the story of Fand and Manannán, and employed him to lure to her an earthly hero to take his place. In any case, it is easy to see how the creature of the *fée*, presumably a giant, might be rationalized into her husband or her oppressor.

[2] Important confirmation of the truth of this development is found in the curiously jumbled incident of *La Joie de la Cort* in Chrétien's *Erec*. The lady (represented as an enchantress), who is of course a rationalized *fée*, is said to have persuaded her lover to enter a garden surrounded by a mysterious wall of air, and

There are, then, in stories of the type represented by the *Serglige* and the *Tale of Curoi* but two original Other-World actors of any consequence : the *fée* and the shape-shifter. In the earlier form of tales of this type, the *fée*, we may assume, made use of the shape-shifter to guide the mortal hero on his way to the Other World and to test his valor before he was admitted there. In the form in which they have come down to us, the tendency to represent the fairy man as superior to the *fée* has asserted itself. The shape-shifter is distressed by a powerful enemy, from whom he can be delivered only by a mortal hero. He therefore, of his own accord, seeks out and guides to the Other World the appropriate hero, and as a reward for his services bestows on him the *fée*.

In the later Irish tales of this type, the various appearances of the shape-shifter in his task of luring and directing the hero to the Other World are made as puzzling as possible. This is perhaps chiefly because the actual character of the shape-shifter has been misunderstood or forgotten ; but one cannot help feeling that sometimes mystification has been purposely introduced for the sake of keeping up the suspense and thus retaining the interest of the listener till the very end. Sometimes, at the close of a tale, a phrase or two is added to explain that the various creatures encountered by the hero were in reality different forms of the same Other-World power. More often

---

to have made him swear to remain there with her till a knight shall enter who can overcome him. Erec enters and overthrows the lover, who is of gigantic size. In this story, it will be seen, the opposing warrior is actually subject to the *fée* (practically her creature), just as must have been the case in the more primitive forms of the Celtic Other-World tale, as we have already inferred on other evidence.

The explanation here sketched of the development of Other-World tales of the *Serglige* type has been merely hinted at in previous chapters, and no arguments at all have been based on it. This has been done of set purpose, lest any reader should suppose that the proof that the story of Chrétien's *Ivain* depends on Celtic sources rested in any way on this reconstruction. The entire explanation may be rejected, without interfering in the least with the train of reasoning which has shown that the *Ivain* and tales like the *Serglige* belong to the same special *genre*, and therefore in all probability must be derived from the same sources. The explanation is inserted at this point as a necessary preliminary to the disentanglement of various modern tales which, through centuries of oral transmission before they were written down, have often become extraordinarily confused.

all elucidatory hints are omitted, and the tale appears, at first sight, a mere jumble of disconnected incidents.

A fair example of an Irish tale of this type, which has been preserved only in a modern manuscript, and has suffered the usual confusions incident to constant retelling and careless transcription, is *The Gillie of the Ferule:*

GIOLLA AN FHIUGHA.[1]

The story begins with the appearance of a mysterious stranger, who presents the hero (Murough) with a brace of hounds sent by the Queen of Pride. He then disappears " like the mist of a winter fog or the whiff of a March wind," and no more is heard of him, or of the Queen of Pride and her message.

The next day Murough goes hunting with the strange hounds, and is led by them to a particular spot, where he meets an odd fellow in a black shirt, who asks to be taken into his service. Murough agrees to hire him and to give him as his wages whatever single request he shall ask at the end of a year. What he asks for is a ferule to fit his stick. The only ferule that will serve turns out to be at the bottom of a lake. The upshot of the matter is that Murough is obliged to dive through the lake into *Tír na n-Óg*, which lies below. There he finds that the King of Under-Wave Land has been robbed of all his possessions by a giant, and that the monster is coming that very evening to carry off the king's daughter. Murough slays the giant and rescues the daughter. He is now escorted to the palace of King Under-Wave, where he finds his Gillie of the Ferule sitting on a golden throne with a silver cushion at his feet. After spending what seem to be several days in perpetual feasting, Murough thinks of returning. When he reaches Ireland, he finds that he has been absent a year and a day.

The remarks of Dr. Hyde in his introduction to this tale throw so much light on the matter that I shall quote them at some length: " To those who are unaccustomed to the ways of the traditional Irish story-teller, *The Lad of the Ferule* will appear entirely wanting in sequence, though it really is not altogether so. . . . The reader familiar with Irish story-telling will understand at once that all this

---

[1] Edited, with a translation, by Douglas Hyde, for the Irish Texts Society, London, 1899, under the title of *The Lad of the Ferule.*

machinery of the hounds, the hunting, and the ferule was put in motion by a mysterious being, a god in fact (a similar being appears in some stories as Lugh, and in others as Manannán), to the end that he might save Tír na n-Óg. It is he who appears as the messenger with the two hounds, and an untrue tale about the Queen of Pride. It is he again who, having by means of his hounds placed Murough in a dilemma, takes service with him as his gillie; and it is he who finally entices him down into Tír na n-Óg, and makes use of him to set free the country. *I feel quite certain that this is the way the story would be understood, and was meant to be understood, by all native Irish readers."* [1] (The italics are mine.)

Our study of the older stories enables us to take a step farther and to understand that " the tale about the Queen of Pride " was not originally " untrue " at all. The Queen of Pride [2] is evidently the *fée* whose creature and servant, in an earlier form of the story, the Gillie of the Ferule really was. She no doubt sent him with the gift of the hounds, her object being to entice away the hero upon whom she had fixed her love. She must also have sent him, disguised as a gillie, to take service with Murough, and thus by the device of the Ferule to entrap him into diving into the lake. Probably she also sent out the giant, by combat with whom the hero could prove his valor. In the present form of the tale, the original thread of connection is all but lost, the only clear hint being the casual indication that the Gillie of the Ferule is identical with King Under-Wave.

The Gillie of the Ferule, however, though more or less confused, has not suffered any positive derangement. The same hero, Murough, still runs through the piece, and there is no evidence of any intentional remodelling. The story has apparently reached its present form as a result of successive slight and almost unintentional modifications. There are some Irish tales of this type that have not only suffered from such gradual decay, but have been actually

---

[1] Pp. viii–x.

[2] Dr. Schofield has reminded me of Lady Orguellouse, who several times appears in the romances (e.g. in Chrétien, *Perceval*, ed. Potvin, III, 28, vv. 10,007 ff.) as dwelling in a mysterious castle. The name may come from some Celtic form like this.

remodelled by some stupid but ambitious transcriber. It happens that a tale of this kind, called *The Slothful Gillie*, is of importance in the present investigation because of a remarkable parallel it contains to Iwain's combat at the Fountain Perilous.

The Slothful Gillie will no doubt appear at first entirely disconnected to one who is not familiar with late Irish stories. It has, indeed, been stupidly remodelled in the latter part of the plot, and the original hero has been displaced by another. I must beg the reader, however, not to make up his mind that it is wholly lacking in sequence, even in its present shape, until he has run through at least half-a-dozen late Irish tales of the type to which it belongs,[1] and has observed how commonly different appearances of the same Other-World creature have been misunderstood and represented as separate and entirely unrelated adventures.

The tale of *The Slothful Gillie* exists unfortunately in no manuscript older than the eighteenth century. However, it is certainly at least as old as 1630, for it is mentioned in that year by Keating, the historian.[2] It will be necessary to summarize it at considerable length in order to show fairly its precise character:

---

[1] See, for example, O'Grady, *Silva Gadelica;* Joyce, *Old Celtic Romances.* A good example of a tale containing adventures apparently disconnected but definitely explained at the end as different appearances of the same shape-shifter, evidently an Other-World power, is the *Amadhan Mor* (Kennedy, *Bardic Stories of Ireland*, pp. 151–155). The hero first meets the Gruagach of the Gold Cup. On his drinking from the cup, his legs drop off below the knees. After the disappearance of the Gruagach of the Cup, leaving him in this plight, he is met by the Gruagach of the White Dog, who invites him to *Dun an Oir*, his abode, and promises to get the Gruagach of the Gold Cup into his power, and force him to restore to the hero his legs. The Gruagach of the White Dog now goes out to hunt, charging the hero to guard the palace till he returns. A mysterious stranger enters and is seized by the hero, who refuses, in spite of his struggles, to release him until he reveals who he is. Suddenly the stranger throws off his disguise. He is the Lord of the Gold Fort (*Dun an Oir*), who took the form of the Gruagach of the Gold Cup, and again that of the Gruagach of the White Dog, in order to lead the hero away to visit his land. He of course restores to the hero his legs, and makes them as strong as ever.

[2] See O'Curry, *Lectures on the MS. Materials*, p. 318. As the latter part of *In Gilla Decair* gives, as it seems, the cause of the Battle of Ventry (namely, the carrying off of Taise, daughter of the king of the Greeks), it may be argued

IN GILLA DECAIR.[1]

One day Finn was out hunting with his Fenians, when they saw approaching an ugly black giant "devilish and misshapen," carrying a "black and loathly colored shield, and every limb of him was blacker than a smith's coal." He led, or rather dragged, by an iron chain an enormous horse, which continually baulked and had to be beaten with an iron club that the giant carried. [The club was so large that as the giant dragged it along, its end resting on the ground tore up a track as deep as the furrow a farmer ploughs with a yoke of oxen.]

The big man came into Finn's presence and saluted him. His name is the Slothful Gillie (*Gilla Decair*), and he desires service under Finn. Finn, who never refused anybody, took the fellow into his pay and gave him permission to put his horse with the horses of the Fenians. No sooner, however, had the monstrous horse come among the other horses than it began to lacerate and kill them with its hoofs and teeth. As the Slothful Gillie refused to restrain his animal, Conan caught it by the halter and by the advice of his comrades resolved to mount it and ride till he had broken its furious temper. But the horse refused to move. The Fenians thought that it would not stir till it had on its back a weight equal to that of the big gillie. They therefore climbed up behind Conan to the number of thirteen.

Suddenly the Slothful Gillie set off with the speed of the wind and his big horse followed him. Conan and his comrades attempted to throw themselves off, but they found that their hands and feet stuck fast to the

---

that it is at least as old as the present form of the Finn cycle. Into the vexed question of the age of the Finn saga it is not possible to go. Barbour's *Bruce* (1380) mentions Finn in a way to show that he was well known. Five tales about Finn are mentioned in the celebrated list in the *Book of Leinster* (Hyde, *Literary Hist. of Ireland*, p. 382). Alfred Nutt has argued (*Waifs and Strays*, II, 414), from the fact that no exploits of Finn against the Normans are related, that the Finn tales took their present form before 1066.

[1] Printed by O'Grady, *Silva Gadelica*, I, 258–276 (translation, II, 292–311), from Additional MS. 34,119 in the British Museum, which dates from 1765. The story has also been in great part translated by Joyce, *Old Celtic Romances*, pp. 223–273, from MS. R. I. A. 24. B. 28, written in 1728, with comparison of MS. R. I. A. 23. G. 21, written in 1795. The essential outline of the story is reproduced in the folk-tale printed by Curtin, *Mac Cool, Hard Gillie, and High King* (*Hero-Tales of Ireland*, pp. 514–529). In the summary I have followed O'Grady's translation, except that the passages in brackets are inserted from Joyce.

horse. The Fenians pursued, and Liagán the Swift managed to seize the horse's tail, to which, however, his hands stuck, and he was dragged along. The horse presently set foot on the sea, across which he travelled till the Fenians lost sight of him.

Finn resolved to follow the fifteen men who had thus been carried away. Two skillful companions met him. One, the ship-maker, produced a magic boat by striking three strokes of his axe on a sling-stick that he had. The other, the sea-tracker, was able to follow the trail of the horse across the unknown sea.

After a three days' voyage [in which they encountered a great storm] Finn and his comrades came to the foot of a precipice [towering to such a height that its head seemed hidden among the clouds], up which the sea-tracker informed them the trail of the big horse led. The voyagers now appealed to Diarmaid, saying that he had been brought up and taught by Manannán mac Lir in the Land of Promise, and that it was a shame if he could not help them. Stung by their words, Diarmaid vaulted by means of his spear-shaft from the ship to the cliff and with great exertion made his way to the top.

Diarmaid advanced alone through a waste and tangled woodland of densest thicket, which of all that he had ever ranged did most abound in foliage, in melody of birds, and in the hum of bees. He was aware of " a vast tree with interlacing boughs and thickly furnished." Close by the tree was a pillar stone provided with a pointed drinking cup and having at its base a fair well of water, clear as crystal [that bubbled up in the centre]. [Twice Diarmaid stooped to drink of the water with his lips, but each time he heard the heavy tread of a body of warriors and the clang of arms, which caused him to spring to his feet. The third time, however, he drank, using the drinking horn, which was chased with gold and enamelled with precious stones.] Scarcely had he put down the horn when he saw a Gruagach approaching, [clad in mail and wearing a scarlet mantle over his armor.] He did not greet Diarmaid, but upbraided him outrageously for roaming his forest and drinking of his fountain. Diarmaid and the Gruagach encountered each other vehemently and fought till sunset. Toward evening the Gruagach drew suddenly back, dived into the well, and disappeared. Next day the contest was renewed, and ended in the same manner. But at the close of the third day, when the Gruagach sought to dive, Diarmaid clasped his arm round him and sank with him to the bottom of the well. Arrived there, the Gruagach broke away. Diarmaid pursued and found himself in an open country, beautiful and flowery. He came to a city, which he entered, passing on to a citadel, " through the portal of which his enemy passed into a place of strength and on him they shut the fortress-gates." Diarmaid fought with a host who were outside and slew them all. Then he lay down to sleep.

He was awakened by a Gruagach, who escorted him to his palace and royally entertained him, healing his wounds and giving him splendid garments. He told Diarmaid that this is Under-Wave Land (*Tír fá Thuinn*). The warrior with whom Diarmaid fought is called the Gruagach of the Well and is the King of Under-Wave Land. His own name is the Gruagach of Chivalry, and he has reason to be kind to Diarmaid, for he once spent a year in the service of Finn Mac Cool in Ireland. There is war between him and the Gruagach of the Fountain.

Diarmaid, on hearing this, agreed to fight for the Gruagach of Chivalry. He slew his old adversary, the Gruagach of the Fountain, and won for his friend the kingship over Under-Wave Land.

Meanwhile Finn and his folk had found their way up the cliff. They fell in with the King of Sorcha, who entertained them. The King of Sorcha was at war with the King of the Greeks and besought Finn to help him. A single combat was at length appointed between Finn and the son of the King of the Greeks. The maiden daughter of the King of the Greeks, Taise of the White Body, had fallen in love with Finn, and she obtained leave of her father to witness the duel. Finn slew his opponent. "Great as was the love which at the first Taise of the White Body had borne Finn, seven times so much she bestowed on him while he butchered her brother."

That night Taise stole away to Finn. But the King of the Greeks heard of it and sent his messenger " provided with a certain special branch of great beauty, which when shaken threw the host into a trance of slumber." By the aid of the mysterious branch, the messenger was able to carry off Taise from the midst of the host of the Fenians. The king thereupon took his daughter and returned to Greece.

Diarmaid now came up, and Finn was rejoiced to learn of his successful adventure. Diarmaid told Finn that the Gruagach of Chivalry had revealed by his magic art that it was Avartach, son of Allchad [of the Many-Colored Raiment[1] who took the form of the Slothful Gillie and] carried away the fifteen Fenians into the Land of Promise.

---

[1] "Avartach mac Allchaid Ioldathach." This Avartach of the Many-Colored Raiment is mentioned along with Manannán mac Lir in *The Pursuit of Diarmuid and Grainne* (ed. Soc. for the Preserv. of Irish, Dublin, 1880, I, 52), where also Ilbhreac (" the variously spotted one "), son of Manannán, is referred to. This connection with Manannán seems to make it clear that the epithets *Ioldathach*, *Ilbreac* refer to shape-shifting, or change of color and form.

Finn and his comrades thereupon made their way to the Land of Promise and recovered their companions. Avartach received them like a king and made them reparation.

Before the Fenians returned to Ireland, Goll and Oscar were sent to Athens, where they stole away Taise and brought her back to Finn. The story ends with the wedding feast of Finn and Taise.

If the reader will compare this tale of *The Slothful Gillie* with that of *The Gillie of the Ferule*, previously outlined, he will see that they belong to essentially the same type. Both are accounts of the doings of an Other-World being, who visits this earth in disguise and takes service as the gillie of a mortal hero. In both tales, his object is to lure a mortal champion to the Land beneath the Waves. In both tales, *Tír fá Thuinn* is reached by diving, though Diarmaid plunges into a well or fountain instead of into a lake as Murough is said to have done.

Now in *The Gillie of the Ferule*, and in all the older tales of this particular type (such as the *Serglige*, the *Loegaire*, and the story of *Pwyll and Arawn*), the motive impelling the Other-World being to desire the visit of a mortal is oppression at the hands of a mysterious foe, whom only a particular mortal hero can overcome. Analogy suggests that this must have been the case with Avartach, and distinct evidence that such was really the motive of his disguise as the Slothful Gillie is not lacking.

The Gruagach of Chivalry is oppressed by a powerful enemy and welcomes Diarmaid, who does actually slay this foe and thus makes his friend king of all *Tír fá Thuinn*, just as a similar exploit of a mortal hero made Fiachna king of all Mag Mell, and Arawn king of all Annwn. Who is this Gruagach of Chivalry, whose name suggests that he is somebody in disguise? All we know about him is that "he has good reason to be kind to Diarmaid, for he once spent a year in the service of Finn." Now Avartach, in the shape of the Slothful Gillie, was for a time in the service of Finn. Clearly the Gruagach of Chivalry is only Avartach in another disguise.[1] The

---

[1] The last transcriber of *In Gilla Decair* has not understood this identity or he would not have said "a year," for the Slothful Gillie is not represented as being in Finn's service for any length of time.

travellers do not find out who he is until they reach his palace, just as Murough does not seem, even after he has reached the Other World, to recognize his Gillie of the Ferule until he enters his palace and sees him sitting on his golden throne. That the Gruagach of Chivalry is identical with Avartach is confirmed by the remark, " It was the Gruagach of Chivalry who revealed by his magic art that it was Avartach of the Many-Colored Raiment who took the form of the Slothful Gillie and carried off the fifteen Fenians into *Tír Tairngiri*," which would mean that he revealed to him that " it was himself, the shape-shifter, who came in the form of the Slothful Gillie." No reader of Irish tales can have much doubt on this point. Analogous situations are not uncommon. In the *Amadhan Mor*, for example, the Gruagach of the White Dog and the Gruagach of the Gold Cup are two forms of the same Other-World being, yet the Gruagach of the White Dog tells the hero that " he will get the Gruagach of the Gold Cup into his power and force him to restore the hero's legs." No other hint of their identity is given till the very end of the tale. Such an explanation at the end, if it ever existed in the *Gilla Decair*, may readily have dropped out in the evident working-over which that part of the tale has undergone. If the Gruagach of Chivalry is identical with Avartach, it is plain that the coming of the Slothful Gillie was really to secure assistance against the Gruagach of the Fountain, and the parallelism with the *Giolla an Fhiugha* and the older tales is complete.

Whether this particular parallel can be regarded as established or not, the fact that the *Gilla Decair* is an Other-World story of the type of the *Giolla an Fhiugha*, and therefore of the *Serglige*, the *Loegaire*, the *Tale of Curoi*, and the tale of *Pwyll and Arawn*, seems certain. The character of Avartach,[1] a confessed shape-shifter, who is called " the man of the many-colored raiment," is enough by itself, in view of the evident Other-World character of the story, to decide

---

[1] It would be natural to suppose that some connection must exist between *Avartach* and *Avallach*, the Welsh name both for the Other World and for the King of the Other World, were it not that the phonetic change of Welsh *ll* to Irish *rt* is contrary to rule. The two names, however, as pronounced, would sound very nearly alike.

this. The *Gilla Decair*, then, belongs to the particular type of Other-World tale to which, as has been shown, Chrétien's *Ivain*, even in its present form, closely approximates. We might expect, therefore, that a study of *In Gilla Decair* would throw light on the rather confusedly rationalized tale of Iwain.

It will be remembered that the theme of the Giant Herdsman in the *Ivain* is distinctly traceable in the older *Mailduin*,[1] and that the original function of this ugly monster was doubtless to point out the way to the Other World. Is it not more than a mere coincidence that in *In Gilla Decair* the black giant with the enormous horse comes expressly to guide the heroes to the Other World? The descriptions of these two monsters are strikingly similar:

In Gilla Decair.	Ivain.
An ugly creature, devilish and misshapen, carrying a black and loathly colored shield, and every limb of him was blacker than a smith's coal. He dragged on the ground an iron club so great that it tore up a track as deep as the furrow a farmer ploughs with a yoke of oxen.	A monstrous and hideous churl, who resembled a Moor and was so ugly that he could not be described. This creature sat on a stump, holding a great club in his hand. He had a head larger than that of a horse, etc.

The Slothful Gillie is not, to be sure, represented as a herdsman in charge of fighting bulls, but he does possess a fighting animal of his own. His enormous horse, when let loose among the horses of the Fenians, "began to lacerate and kill them with its hoofs and teeth." It will be remembered that in the *Mailduin* we have found the Giant Herdsman motive represented (§ 9) by "many great animals like unto horses which were fighting each other. Each would take a piece out of another's side and carry it away with its skin and its flesh, so that out of their sides streams of crimson blood were flowing."[2] In an older form of the theme, the monstrous animals

---

[1] See p. 73, above.   [2] See p. 61, above.

may well have been more like horses than bulls. The change to cattle would be a step toward rationalization, for a cattle-driver was a not uncommon object.[1]

Now the Slothful Gillie we know to have been Avartach, an Other-World being in disguise. By analogy, therefore, we are able to explain the presence of the Giant Herdsman in the *Ivain*. He was originally the creature of the *fée*, sent by her to guide the hero to the Other World.

---

[1] Of course it is only contended that the Slothful Gillie and the Giant Herdsman may go back to the same stock incident of the Celtic Journey to the Other World. If the Slothful Gillie theme be founded on the Giant Herdsman motive, it has certainly experienced an entirely different development. The idea of representing the Gillie's horse as *carrying* off certain mortals to the Other World is no doubt the result of contamination with another theme, which, however, is itself almost certainly Celtic. In the earliest tales (the *Serglige*, the *Bran*) Manannán is seen driving in a chariot over the sea, while in the *Story of Ciabán* we have found him carrying the heroes on the back of his horse to the Land beyond the Waves. Avartach is a parallel figure to Manannán, and it is natural to have him turn up with a steed like Manannán's horse *Enbarr*, which travelled equally well by sea or by land (see p. 42, note, above) The use of horses to return from the Other World appears in the ancient *Tale of Loegaire* (cf. the Welsh Herla), and the use of a magic steed to reach the Other World appears constantly in modern Celtic folk-tales. The motive is, therefore, almost certainly ancient Celtic.

The incident of cleaving fast to an object and being carried off with it to the Other World is perhaps also Celtic. In the Mabinogi *Manawyddan Son of Llyr* (Loth, *Les Mabinogion*, I, 106), Pryderi and Rhiannon enter a mysterious palace, and place their hands on a bowl they find there. Their hands immediately stick, so that they cannot escape. The palace presently vanishes, and Pryderi and Rhiannon are found to have been carried to the Other World. The incident of successive riders who mount the same horse and are all stuck fast and carried off into a lake occurs in a modern Golspie tale (Nicholson, *Golspie*, London, 1897, pp. 21–23; a reference which I owe to Professor Kittredge). No one would maintain that the motive of magically adhering to an object is of especially Celtic origin. In *The Chase of Slieve Fuad* (Joyce, *Old Celtic Romances*, p. 376), the heroes cleave to the floor of the Other-World dungeon of the giant Dryantore. In the *Fairy Palace of the Quicken Trees* (Joyce, p. 193), Finn and his comrades cleave to their seats so that they cannot arise. See J. F. Campbell, *Popular Tales of the West Highlands*, I, 36; MacDougall, *Folk and Hero Tales*, p. 164; and, outside of Celtic ground, *The Tale of the Basyn*, Hazlitt, *Early Popular Poetry of England*, III, 42–53; the Prose Edda, *Bragarœður*, chap. 56. Vulcan also had a seat from which nobody could arise (Prato, *Zt. f. Volkskunde*, I, 113).

In the *Gilla Decair*, the Other-World power Avartach comes in the shape of a black giant to lure the Fenians to *Tír fá Thuinn*. Diarmaid, who has been trained up by Manannán, actually reaches Under-Wave Land, and frees Avartach, who appears under the name of the Gruagach of Chivalry, from an oppressing tyrant, the Gruagach of the Fountain. As a reward, he ought, on the analogy of all the older stories, to receive the hand of a *fée*. Instead of that, he drops out of the tale, and Finn is suddenly exalted to the leading position. It is incredible that the tale in any primitive form could have thus changed protagonists at the centre of the action. The story appears, then, to have been confused at this point, and Finn has been introduced in place of Diarmaid. Finn takes sides with the King of Sorcha, an Other-World ruler, and frees him from the oppression of the King of the Greeks. He wins the love of Taise of the White Body, daughter of the King of the Greeks. Taise is evidently a rationalized *fée*. If the analogy of other modern Irish tales, in which the King of the Greeks regularly represents a partly rationalized King of the Fairies (see p. 97, above), were not sufficient to prove this, the magic branch employed by the messenger of the King of the Greeks should settle the point. Parallels to this branch run through the ancient Celtic fairy stories.[1] In a more primitive form of the *Gilla Decair* tale, Finn did probably visit the Other World and encounter there Diarmaid, who had successfully accomplished the Other-World adventure, just as Arthur in the *Ivain* comes to the Fountain Perilous and is entertained at Laudine's castle by the successful hero.[2] Finn ought not, however, to win the hand of

---

[1] See the *Imram Brain* and the *Echtra Cormaic*.

[2] Alfred Nutt (*Voyage of Bran*, I, 140) has drawn a number of parallels between Finn and Arthur. Both have birth stories, *enfances*, unfaithful wives, and traitorous nephews. To this I would add that both made journeys to the Other World, and that Finn's meeting with Diarmaid, who has successfully accomplished the adventure of *Tír fá Thuinn*, is a scene very similar to Arthur's meeting with the successful Iwain at Laudine's castle.

That the attribution to Finn of a journey to the Other World was made very early seems indicated by a poem in the *Book of Leinster* (edited and translated by Stokes, *Rev. Celt.*, VII, 289–307), which describes the visit of Finn and his companions to a land of monstrous beings, with whom they have an all-night

the *fée*. It is Diarmaid, not Finn, who was brought up in the Land
of Promise by Manannán mac Lir, and who was thus specially educated, as it were, for the Other-World adventure. It is Diarmaid,
"the best lover of women and maidens in the whole world," [1] —
Diarmaid, who had a beauty spot that made every woman who saw
it fall in love with him, — who would naturally win the *fée*. Moreover, there are numbers of later tales that represent Diarmaid as the
hero of a fairy mistress story.[2] Hence it is probable that, as Conan,

---

combat. Alfred Nutt (*Waifs and Strays*, IV, 11, 283) has given a reference to
Dunbar which shows that in the time of the poet (1450–1525) Finn or Finn's
followers were credited with harrowing hell.

[1] *The Pursuit of Diarmuid and Grainne* (ed. Soc. for the Preserv. of Irish,
1880, I, 7).

[2] In a modern folk-tale, *Dyeermud Ulta and the King in South Erin* (Curtin,
Hero-Tales, pp. 182 ff., from County Donegal), Dyeermud sees a red champion in
a ship that is sailing along the country like any ship at sea. (The Other-World
ship, like the Other-World horse, regularly travels by land as well as by sea: cf.
Bran, § 42; *Mailduin*, § 23; and a passage from the *Book of Leinster*, translated
by O'Grady, *Silva Gadelica*, II, 453, where three ships navigating the air over
men's heads are described.) By the aid of the red champion, Dyeermud is able
to sail up to a castle situated twenty miles from the sea, the lord of which had
declared that he would give his daughter to nobody except the man who could
come to his castle gate in a three-masted ship. After overcoming the lord of the
castle, Dyeermud marries his daughter. In a West Highland tale (Campbell, III,
403–420), Diarmaid visits the Other World and marries the daughter of King
Under-Wave.

In a modern Irish tale, *Fin Mac Cool, Faolan, and the Mountain of Happiness*
(Curtin, *Hero-Tales*, pp. 489 ff., from County Kerry), Dyeermud wins a fairy
mistress from a revolving castle after having first overcome the Black Blue Giant,
her father. This giant is said "to know every place in the world," so that he is
probably an enchanter like Avartach, and his name (Black Blue) is probably a
reference to his power of changing color and shape. Curiously enough it is said
that the giant's daughter was already in love with Dyeermud, having seen him
once in combat with the Prince of the Greeks on Ventry Strand. It will be
remembered that, in the *Gilla Decair*, Taise falls in love with Finn when she sees
him in combat with the Prince of the Greeks, her brother. It is possible to hold
that the stories refer to the same incident, and that the modern tale of Dyeermud
has preserved the original situation in the *Gilla Decair*, of which all analogy shows
Diarmaid must once have been the hero. Nor is the ascription of the Other-
World adventure to Diarmaid a modern idea. *The Pursuit of Diarmuid and
Grainne* is mentioned in the list of stories given in the *Book of Leinster* (Hyde,

the backbiter of the Finn cycle, was a parallel figure to Kay, so Diarmaid was a parallel figure to Iwain (or Gawain) as its typical Other-World adventurer.

We cannot be quite sure what has happened to the tale of the *Gilla Decair* at the point where Diarmaid drops out of sight,[1] but it seems probable that Finn has been inserted in place of his follower. In the original form of the story, then, we must infer that Taise the *fée* fell in love with Diarmaid. She sent Avartach, the shape-shifter, in the form of the Slothful Gillie, to lure the Fenians to her land. She then appointed another of her creatures, the Gruagach of the Fountain, to encounter Diarmaid and test his valor, and only at the last, when the hero had successfully overthrown this Gruagach and other enemies, did she bestow on him her hand. The King of Sorcha must be a later name for Avartach, and the King of the Greeks, for the Gruagach of the Fountain.

Our inference that such was the original form of the tale seems to be supported by the remark: "Great as was at the first the love which Taise of the White Body had borne Finn, seven times so much she bestowed on him while he butchered her brother." "Her brother" was of course not originally a brother at all. He was one of her creatures, sent out to test the hero's valor, like the monsters sent out to attack Cuchulinn at the castle of Curoi. Hence she rejoiced to see the hero conquer him, just as Bláthnat had kind words for Cuchulinn when he entered the fort victorious.[2] We have, indeed, in the rationalized description of the opposing warrior as the lady's brother a parallel to the *Tale of Curoi* and, I may add, to the *Ivain*, where the opponent is called the lady's husband.

Lit. Hist. of Ireland, pp. 350 ff.), and it contains a well-defined Other-World incident of which Diarmaid is the hero. There is a marvellous quicken tree sprung from one of the berries of the Land of Promise and guarded by a giant whom Diarmaid slays (*Pursuit of Diarmuid and Grainne*, ed. Soc. for Preserv. of Irish, 1880, I, 53 ff.); cf. *Lay of Diarmaid*, J. F. Campbell, *Popular Tales of the West Highlands*, III, 50 ff.

[1] It is quite possible, for example, that a fairy mistress story about Finn has been worked into the *Gilla Decair*, and substituted for the original adventures of Diarmaid.

[2] See p. 51, above.

If this reconstruction be sound, — and it is supported by the analogy both of ancient and of later Celtic stories, — we are able, by comparison, to see the original thread on which were strung together several adventures of the *Ivain* that have hitherto seemed rather disconnected.   The Giant Herdsman, and probably therefore the Hospitable Host, must originally have been different appearances of the same Other-World being,[1] a shape-shifter commissioned by the *fée* to guide the hero to her land.   The story must once have run somewhat as follows: The *fée*, Laudine, fell in love with Iwain, and sent her attendant maiden Lunete to Arthur's court to invite the visit of mortal heroes.   Calogrenant was the first to accept, but, not being the chosen one, he returned in discomfiture.   At last Iwain set out.   The Hospitable Host is the creature of the *fée* appointed to further his journey.   The Giant Herdsman is another appearance of the same shape-shifter, designed to point out the particular path that leads to the Other World.   Esclados le Ros was at first also only another of the *fée's* creatures, whose object was to try the hero's valor.   If the hero overcame this mysterious giant, he was to be rewarded with the hand of the *fée*.   This last situation was very early misunderstood, and probably long before the material reached Chrétien had been changed into a combat with the lady's husband.   Thus by natural steps may have arisen that theme of the sudden marriage of a newly bereaved widow to the slayer of her husband which has been such a puzzle to the critics.

However, it is not necessary to postulate any of the theories just outlined in order to prove that the *Gilla Decair* belongs to that type of Other-World adventure of which the *Serglige Conculaind* is a good example.   Nor is it even necessary to accept the plausible reconstruction of the *Gilla Decair* story which would retain Diarmaid as the hero throughout.   Putting aside every particle of theory, and comparing the *Gilla Decair*, just as it is, with stories like the *Serglige*, the *Loegaire*, and the *Tale of Curoi*, I do not see how it is possible to avoid the conviction that these stories all belong to the same

---

[1] Baist, *Zt. f. rom. Phil.*, XXI, 403, has remarked that the Hospitable Host and the Giant Herdsman may originally have had some more intimate connection with the adventure than any which appears in the *Ivain.*

type. Like the rest, the *Gilla Decair* is an Other-World Journey. As in the other stories, the visit of the mortal heroes was invited and a combat in the Other World is a central incident. Above all, the character of Avartach, so strikingly similar to that of Manannán, of Arawn, and of Curoi, puts the identity of type beyond a reasonable doubt.

The tale of the *Gilla Decair*, then, belongs to a type to which it has been shown that Chrétien's *Ivain* closely approximates. It is natural, therefore, to expect to find in it certain of the stock motives of the Celtic Other-World Journey preserved in a form very like that in which they occur in the *Ivain*. And this is exactly what we seem to find. As has been said, the parallel that it contains to the whole scene of the combat at the Fountain Perilous is of the most significant character:

1. In both tales, the hero finds tangled woods of densest thicket:

> Et trovai un chemin a destre
> Parmi une forest espesse.
> Mout i ot voie felenesse,
> De ronces et d'espines plainne (vv. 180 ff.).

2. In both, he hears the song of birds:

> Et trestuit li oisel chantoient
> Si que trestuit s'antracordoient (vv. 465–466).

3. In both, there is a vast tree:

> Onbre li fet li plus biaus (or *hauz*) arbres
> Qu'onques poïst feire nature (vv. 382–383).

4. With thickly interlacing boughs:

> Que ce estoit li plus biaus pins
> Qui onques sor terre creüst.
> Ne cuit qu'onques si fort pleüst
> Que d'iaue i passast une gote (vv. 414 ff.).

5. And there is a notable stone:

> Un perron tel con tu verras (v. 390).

6. To which belongs a golden drinking vessel:

> A l'arbre vi le bacin pandre
> Del plus fin or qui fust a vandre
> Onques ancor an nule foire (vv. 419 ff.).

7. Immediately beneath the tree, and beside the stone, there is a bubbling spring :

> De la fontainne poez croire
> Qu'ele boloit com iaue chaude (vv. 422, 423).

8. In both stories, troubling the fountain provokes the appearance of a hostile warrior, who makes so much noise with his armor that before he appears the hero thinks a whole band of armed men is approaching :

> Tant i fui que j'oï venir
> Chevaliers, ce me fu avis —
> Bien cuidai que il fussent dis :
> Tel noise et tel fraint demenoit
> Uns seus chevaliers qui venoit (vv. 478 ff.).

Compare
> Li chevaliers a si grant bruit
> Con s'il chaçast un cerf de ruit (vv. 813–814).

9. In both tales, the warrior does not greet the hero, but reproaches him vehemently for damaging his dominions :

> De si haut com il pot criër,
> Me comança a desfiër, etc. (vv. 489 ff.).

10. This warrior is in one tale clad in red, and in the other is called

> Esclados le Ros (v. 1970).

11. In both, the hero overcomes his adversary, and, pursuing him, enters into a magic land.

12. In both, the escaping warrior flees through the streets of a city and enters a citadel, the gates of which are shut behind him.

It is clear that a whole chapter, so to speak, out of the *Gilla Decair* is strikingly similar both in incident and in arrangement to a corresponding portion of the *Ivain*. The resemblances, it will be noted, sometimes extend to very minute details, such as the interlacing boughs of the tree and the clatter made by the approaching warrior.

Several scholars[1] have pointed out the practical identity of this

---

[1] Macbain, *Celtic Magazine*, IX, 278 (1884) ; Alfred Nutt, *Celtic Magazine*, XII, 555 (1887); Rhŷs, *Hibbert Lectures*, pp. 187 ff. (1888); F. Lot, *Romania*, XXI, 67 ff. (1892). No one of the last three scholars refers to any of his predecessors.

episode in the *Gilla Decair* with the adventure at the Fountain in the *Ivain*, and Ferdinand Lot has summed up the situation thus: "En résumé, nous sommes en présence de trois hypothèses : 1° ou bien ce thème est irlandais, et alors son origine celtique est patente ; 2° ou bien il est emprunté à quelque poète français (Chrétien ou autre) ; je n'insiste pas sur cette supposition qui me paraît chimérique ; 3° Chrétien de Troyes et le conte irlandais ont une source commune, et cette source est quelque légende galloise. La première hypothèse me paraît, quant à moi, la plus vraisemblable. En tout cas, ce thème est celtique, bien celtique, et c'est une nouvelle preuve de l'origine celtique des récits utilisés par Chrétien." [1]

Lot, though recognizing the probability that the theme is really Celtic, made no systematic effort to disprove the second hypothesis, which he mentioned but for himself rejected. The limits of his article did not permit him to study the ways of the later Irish story-teller,[2] and to show that the present confused form of the *Gilla Decair* story may well be the result of the dislocation of an ancient Celtic Other-World tale.

To one who has followed the development of stories of this type from the *Serglige* to *The Gillie of the Ferule*, Lot's second hypothesis must seem altogether untenable. There are several incidents in the episode under discussion which cannot have been taken from Chrétien, and are indeed more primitive than the corresponding features of the account in the *Ivain*. The challenge by drinking at a fountain is a simpler and older form of the motive than that by pouring water on a rock and thus provoking a furious storm.[3] Diarmaid's diving beneath the water in order to reach *Tír fá Thuinn* is a

---

[1] *Romania*, XXI, 71.

[2] Lot says (p. 71): "Cet épisode semble intercalé dans la *Poursuite de Gilla Dacker*, car il n'est pas utile au reste du récit." He adds a note, however, which shows that he had not rejected the possibility of a different explanation : "Cependant je n'en répondrais pas absolument. Presque toutes les légendes irlandaises nous semblent se composer d'épisodes qui ne se rattachent pas nettement les uns aux autres ; c'est du moins l'impression qu'elles produisent sur nous autres Français, qui voulons une certaine suite, même dans le fantastique."

[3] Lot has noted this.

very ancient motive, which can hardly have been the insertion of
a late copyist.   Loegaire, according to the *Book of Leinster*, plunged
into a loch to reach Mag Mell.   In the *Fled Bricrend*, Terror, who
is a mere duplicate of Curoi, departed *into the loch*, and in *The Gillie
of the Ferule*, Murough reached Under-Wave Land by diving into a
lake.   The incident appears to be a survival.

To pass over these apparent survivals of primitive incidents, the
real point that makes the theory of borrowing impossible is this:
How could a late compiler, who *ex hypothesi* knew nothing of the
real character of the *Ivain*, have had the miraculous fortune to insert
his extract from Chrétien into exactly that type of story to which
investigation makes it clear that the *Ivain* originally belonged?   Is
it by chance that the adventure is attributed to Diarmaid, who was
trained up by Manannán mac Lir and was well. understood to be
the Other-World adventurer of the Finn cycle?   And, above all, is
it by chance that Avartach is introduced into the story, — a figure
exactly parallel to Manannán, to Arawn, to Curoi, and to the Other-
World actor who must have played an important part in an older
form of the tale of Iwain?   No matter what views one may entertain as to the precise make-up of the *Gilla Decair*, the chances
against such an hypothesis as this are enormous.

This episode in the *Gilla Decair* must, then, be a survival of a
primitive Celtic theme which long ago made its way into French
literature and has been preserved in the *Ivain*.   The Celtic origin
of the main portion of Chrétien's poem is therefore settled beyond
dispute.

It must not be supposed, however, that the proof of the dependence of the *Ivain* on a Celtic story of the type conveniently represented by the *Serglige* rests in any way on the *Gilla Decair*.   The
present chapter, dealing with the later Irish stories, has been written
only with the intention of confirming an hypothesis already put
practically beyond the reach of doubt by the ancient documents.
We have found in the more modern Irish literature just those resemblances to the *Ivain* that one might expect if the theory of Celtic
origin be true.   The case, however, really rests on the ancient
tales.   Therefore, even if it should at some time be proved that
the striking resemblances between the *Gilla Decair* and the *Ivain*

are due to a knowledge of Chrétien's poem, the argument for the Celtic origin of the *Ivain* would not be sensibly weakened, much less overthrown.[1]

CHAPTER VI.

·IWAIN IN THE OTHER WORLD.

To prove a basis in Celtic tradition for the story of Chrétien's *Ivain*, the supposition that the particular hero, after whom the romance is named, was well known among the Celts as an Other-World adventurer is not a necessary prerequisite. The Other-World story was told of various heroes from Connla to the Welsh Herla, and it may not have got attached to Iwain till very shortly before the time of Chrétien.

Even if our information about Celtic legend were tolerably complete (which is not the case), a critic who should urge that, because Iwain does not in any extant Celtic story appear as an Other-World adventurer, therefore Chrétien's romance called *Ivain* cannot go back to Celtic sources, would be making a very weak objection indeed.

---

[1] All possibility of the influence of Chrétien on the episode in the *Gilla Decair* seems, however, practically excluded. The only hypothesis of this sort that is rationally thinkable, so far as I can see, is that the *Gilla Decair* story, in an earlier form, possessed an incident so similar to that at the Fountain Perilous that some Irish transcriber who was familiar with Chrétien (there is a late Irish version of the *Ivain*, *Echtra Ridire na Leoman*, in an eighteenth-century MS., H. 2. 6, at Trinity College, Dublin; see Zimmer, *Gött. Gel. Anz.*, 1890, p. 510) noticed the resemblance and modified his original in places in order to produce that practical identity of detail that we now observe. A transcriber, however, who worked in this way would probably have made the resemblance complete. He would surely, for example, have omitted the dive into the fountain. Besides, this is really a question-begging hypothesis, after all, for either the transcriber must have been a man of such supernatural insight that he could anticipate the results of modern investigation, or the resemblances even in the first place must have been so striking that a presumably not over-intelligent Irishman of several centuries ago could easily recognize them. Surely, if either of these alternatives be granted, it is all that any advocate of the Celtic theory need desire.

He would be assuming that a story never changes its protagonist. The truth is quite otherwise. A student of literary origins early learns that, although incidents survive and may be safely used to trace a source, the name of the hero of any particular incident changes with considerable facility.[1] In the present discussion, therefore, any argument that should depend for its validity upon the assumed persistence of a single proper name has been, and ought to be as far as possible, excluded.

Notwithstanding this fact, it is worth while to observe that the inherent probability that Owen, who was one of the best known and most celebrated heroes of the Welsh,[2] became in popular legend an Other-World adventurer, is supported by the circumstance that several French romances contain incidents plainly of Celtic origin in which Iwain is associated with the Other World. Of course these incidents *prove* nothing, because Iwain may not have been their original hero, but they are interesting, and they will be cited since they serve to establish a kind of presumption that Iwain was well known as an Other-World adventurer.

In the *Bataille Loquifer*,[3] a twelfth-century romance, three *fées* appear and say: "Let us carry Rainouart to Avalon and make him live in the midst of our friends, King Arthur, Yvain de Galles, Gauvain, and Roland." Rainouart is accordingly borne to Avalon, where he is made to fight the cat Chapalu.

In the prose *Lancelot*,[4] Iwain appears as a prisoner in a mysterious castle.[5] He is detained by Morgain la Fée. The region where the castle is located is called "Le Val sans Retour" and can be reached

---

[1] Compare, to mention well-known examples only, how in the Arthurian romances Galahad usurped the position of Grail Hero, earlier assigned to Perceval ; and in the *chansons de geste*, how Charlemagne became the central figure of adventures originally belonging to Charles Martel and Charles the Bald.

[2] For evidence of the early and great popularity of Owen among the Welsh, see Skene, *Four Ancient Books of Wales*, index, s.v. *Owen*.

[3] See *Hist. Litt.*, XXII, 535–536.

[4] P. Paris, *Les Romans de la Table Ronde*, IV, *Lancelot du Lac*, pp. 283–293. Cf. III, 362, where Yvain is prisoner to Morganor.

[5] In *Claris et Laris* (ed. Alton, pp. 17 ff.), a thirteenth-century romance, Iwain is released from prison by Claris and Laris. This is perhaps a rationalization of the incident discussed above.

only by a narrow passage, guarded by five armed knights. Lancelot traverses the difficult passage, overthrows the knights, passes a wall of flames, ascends a staircase guarded by three warriors, and is at last successful in releasing Iwain and the other prisoners of Morgain. When the prisoners are released, Le Val sans Retour, its castles, its walls, its warriors, and its enchantments suddenly vanish.

This "Val sans Retour" appears to be identical with the place described in Chrétien's *Lancelot* as Meleagant's prison. Meleagant's prison was in the realm "don nus n'eschape,"[1] and could be reached only by two mysterious bridges, one passing under water and the other consisting of a sharp sword. The prisoners in it were likewise released by Lancelot.

Meleagant's prison, as Paris has shown,[2] is really the Other World, the Land of the Dead.[3] It is highly probable, therefore, that this

---

[1] Ed. Foerster, *Der Karrenritter*, 1899, v. 1948; cf. vv. 657 ff.

[2] *Romania*, XII, 459–534.

[3] Compare a passage in Chrétien's *Lancelot* where there is a cemetery described, full of tombs, upon the covers of which are inscribed the names of those who are to lie there. Lancelot enters:

> Comança les letres a lire,
> Et trova: "Ci girra Gauvains,
> Ci Looys et ci Yvains."
> Aprés cez trois i a mainz liz
> Des nons des chevaliers esliz,
> Des plus prisiez et des meillors
> Et de cele terre et d'aillors (vv. 1876 ff.).

Lancelot comes at length to a marble tomb, more beautiful than the others, on which is written:

> Cil qui levera
> Ceste lame seus par son cors,
> Getera ceus et celes fors,
> Qui sont an la terre an prison (vv. 1912 ff.).

To the intense astonishment of his guide, Lancelot is able to raise the cover of this tomb. He is thereupon told that he is the destined one

> qui deliverra
> Toz ces qui sont pris a la trape
> El reaume don nus n'eschape (vv. 1946 ff.).

This story is obscurely told, but it appears possible that it, too, is a confused rationalization of some more primitive incident in which Iwain was represented as imprisoned in the Other World.

imprisonment of Iwain in " Le Val sans Retour" described in the
prose *Lancelot* is a partial rationalization of some older story that
represented Iwain as having undertaken a journey to the Other
World.   It is exactly what would be expected if Iwain was, among
the Celts, a well-known Other-World adventurer, like Connla or
Cuchulinn.   From the *Adventures of Teigue* (p. 74, above) it is plain
that Connla was thought of as living in the Other World.   Stories
representing Iwain as dwelling in Avalon or in the Realm of the
Dead might easily find their way into the French romances.

In view of this fact, one is tempted to suggest that Owain Miles,
the legend of whose journey to Purgatory and Paradise appeared in
the twelfth century [1] and made its way into almost all the literatures
of Western Europe, is really the same person as Sir Iwain, Arthur's
knight,[2] and that the visit to Purgatory was ascribed to him because
of his well-known connection with the Other World.   Nothing is
easier than the transition from the Celtic Other World to the
Christian Purgatory and Paradise.   As has been said in a previous
chapter, the Happy Other World became confused with the Christian
Earthly Paradise.   This identification once under way, a connection
with Purgatory, a place of punishment, would not be difficult.[3]   The
story of *Owain Miles*, moreover, though based in general on the
widely spread Christian vision-literature of the Middle Ages, differs
from the mediæval type to which it belongs in several features, which
seem to show the influence of Celtic Other-World journey.

While the typical visit to Purgatory and Paradise is a vision and
the narrator has no idea of the road by which he travelled, it is clear

---

[1] The first mention of the Purgatory of St. Patrick is made by the monk Jocelin
of Furness in his *Vita Sancti Patricii* (about 1183).   The oldest account of a
journey through the cavern called the Purgatory of St. Patrick is the *Tractatus de
Purgatorio Sancti Patricii*, written by H[enry?] of Saltrey, probably about 1188.
From this Latin *Tractatus*, Marie's *Espurgatoire*, the English *Owain Miles*, and
other versions are derived (see Jenkins, *L'Espurgatoire of Marie*, pp. 1 ff.).   See
also E. J. Becker, *Contrib. to the Comp. Study of the Med. Visions*, etc., 1899;
G. P. Knapp, *St. Patrick's Purgatory*, 1900.

[2] This suggestion was made in 1820 by Roquefort, *Marie de France*, II, 405.

[3] Confusion of fairyland with hell and of the fairies with evil spirits is not
uncommon in later tales.   It is especially frequent in the tales of Brittany (cf. Le
Braz, *La Légende de la Mort*, 1893, pp. 459 ff.), but is often found elsewhere.

that Owain Miles went in the body, and the place by which he entered the Other World is defined exactly. The so-called Purgatory of St. Patrick is a cave situated upon an island in Lough Dearg, County Donegal, Ireland. Moreover, Owain is described as a soldier [1]: "Contigit autem hijs nostris temporibus, diebus scilicet Regis stephani, ut miles quidam nomine Owein [MS. K also reads *Owein*], de quo presens est narratio," etc. He has been an exceedingly wicked man, but has repented, and as a penance has resolved to enter the Purgatory. He is conducted thither by the monks of the place, who sing a solemn service over him. They warn him earnestly of the peril of the adventure, but he is described as " vir virilem in pectore gerens animum . . . qui ergo armis munitus ferreis bellis interfuerat hominum quam plurimis, fide, spe et justitia armatus ad pugnam audacter prorumpit demonum." [2]

It is evident that Owain has been a great warrior, a circumstance not usual in mediæval vision-literature. It is therefore possible that the epithet " Miles " may be a survival of his knightly character.[8]

Owain's adventures in Purgatory have no similarity to the incidents of Celtic Other-World journeys, but when he has passed this dismal region, he finds that the entrance to *Paradisus Terrestris* lies across a narrow bridge that may show traces of Celtic influence:

> The brigge was as heighe as a tour
> And as scharpe as a rasour
> And naru it was also,
> And the water that ther ran under
> Brend o lighting and of thonder,
> That thought him michel wo.[4]

---

[1] Quoted from Mall's edition of the *Tractatus*, MS. A (*Romanische Forschungen*, VI, 153). For a somewhat different version of Owain's journey, see Matthew Paris, *Chronica Majora*, ed. Luard, Rolls Series, II, 192–203.   [2] Ed. Mall, p. 156.

[8] *Miles* is a common word for "knight" in records and other documents. Cf. *Launfal Miles*, the title of Thomas Chestre's well-known poem.

[4] Quoted from the English *Owain Miles*, a rare edition (limited to thirty-two copies) published from the Auchinleck MS., Edinburgh, 1837 (see p. 35). This poem has been edited also by Kölbing, *Englische Studien*, I, 99–112. In the Latin original (ed. Mall, pp. 174–175) the bridge is said to have three difficulties: first, it was very slippery; secondly, it was very narrow; and, thirdly, it was at a

When Owein has entered the Terrestrial Paradise, he finds a land-scape which much resembles that commonly described in Celtic stories of the Journey to the Other World:

> Other joies he seighe anough
> Heighe tres with mani a bough
> Ther on sat foules of heuen,
> And breke her notes with miri gle
> Burdoun and mene gret plente
> And hautain with heighe steven.
> Him thought wele with that foules song
> He might wele liue ther among
> Til the worldes ende.[1]

The high trees, the many birds, and the delicious sweetness of their song, which causes the time to pass quickly, mark this scene as identical with that described in the *Imram Snedgusa* and the *Navigatio Sancti Brandani*.[2]

In view of these similarities to Celtic story, it might at first appear probable that *Owain Miles* is at bottom some Other-World tale about Sir Iwain which has been entirely remodelled and worked over on the pattern of Christian vision-literature. A moment's consideration, however, shows that the Other-World landscape is not a sufficient basis for argument, since it was a conventional part of the description of the Earthly Paradise in Christian visions before the date of

---

dizzy height. Another English poem called *Owayne Miles* (Kölbing, pp. 113–121) describes this bridge thus:

> Ouur þe watur a brygge þer was,
> ffor soþe kener þen ony glasse;
> hyt was narowe and hit was hyȝe,
> oneþe þat oþur ende he syȝe;
> The myddyll was hyȝe, þe ende was lowe,
> hyt ferde, as hyt hadde ben a bent bowe (vv. 413 ff.).

Compare the bridge which Cuchulinn, according to the *Tochmarc Emere*, had to pass on his way to Scáthach's abode. This was low at both ends, high in the middle, and so constructed that, when a man stepped on the one end, the other end would rise aloft, and he would be thrown down (see p. 75, note 1, above).

[1] Ed. of 1837, p. 41. The corresponding passage in the Latin *Tractatus* (ed. Mall, pp. 181 ff.) is by no means so close a parallel to Celtic story.

[2] See pp. 85 ff., above.

the *Tractatus*.[1] Moreover, when one considers that the similarities between *Owain Miles* and Celtic story are almost entirely lacking in the Latin *Tractatus*, it seems more likely that the tale was originally a vision and that the similarities to Celtic story have been introduced later. Any connection, therefore, between Owain Miles and Sir Iwain, Arthur's knight, becomes exceedingly doubtful, especially in view of the fact that Owain or Owen is a very common name among the Welsh.

CHAPTER VII.

CHRÉTIEN'S REDACTION OF THE TALE OF IWAIN.

Not only did Chrétien dress up the story of Iwain in the costume of the age of chivalry, but it is practically certain that he also greatly modified some of the incidents and introduced a number of his own. This is especially true, as has been said, of the latter portion of the *Ivain*.

In the case of the Magic Fountain, which occurs early in the poem, there is no way of being sure that the rain-making qualities of the well may not have been attached to the story, and the fountain localized at Bérenton, before the time of Chrétien.

The Fountain Perilous, as is shown by its connection with the Wonderful Tree and the marvellous singing birds, must be in origin that noble well which is a part of the Other-World landscape in ancient Celtic story. As soon as the supernatural character of this fountain became confused, it might plausibly be described as only a marvellous spring or well existing somewhere on this earth. This change we know actually happened in very early Irish story. In the *Mailduin*, § 20, we find the fountain represented as a religious marvel that gave milk on Sundays and wine on holy days. The fountain of Other-World story once thought of as magical, it would be easy

---

[1] The Other-World landscape appears in the *Visio Tnugdali*, composed before 1160 (see p. 90, above).

for it to be localized and identified with one of the many magic wells that were believed in during the Middle Ages. It is not uncommon for these wells to be represented as rain-making,[1] so that it is likely that such a quality had been connected with the Fountain Perilous before the materials came to the hand of Chrétien. It is clear that in the *Ivain* the Fountain Perilous is meant to be identified with the Fountain of Bérenton in Armorica. Now Wace, writing a few years before Chrétien,[2] described this Fountain of Bérenton, and verbal resemblances seem to show that Chrétien had Wace's account at hand when he was describing the journey of Calogrenant. It is possible, therefore, that the localization of the Fountain Perilous at Bérenton is due to Chrétien, whose interest in the Armorican fountain may have been aroused by the recent narrative of Wace. This inference, however, does not necessarily follow from the fact that Chrétien seems to have borrowed a few phrases from Wace.[8] Even if the material which Chrétien was using already connected with Bérenton the fountain that Iwain visited, the French poet may well

---

[1] Giraldus Cambrensis (1146–1220), in his *Topographia Hiberniae* (dist. ii, cap. 7), describes a fountain in Munster such that if it be touched, or even seen, by a man, forthwith the entire province is inundated by rain. The rain will not cease till a priest is sent to celebrate mass in a chapel which has been built near the fountain. (Cf. other versions of the Wonders of Ireland: see K. Meyer, *Folk-Lore*, V, 304.) This mention of a chapel reminds one of the chapel near the Fountain Perilous in the *Ivain*, where Lunete was confined. It is usual to find the ruins of a chapel near a magic or holy well. See M. and L. Quiller-Couch, *Ancient and Holy Wells of Cornwall*, London, 1894. In Lady Guest's *Mabinogion*, I, 226, there is a modern tale about a lake, near Snowdon in Wales, called Dulyn. If water be dipped from this lake, and poured on a stone called "the red altar," it is rare that rain does not fall before night. In J. M. MacKinlay, *Folklore of the Scottish Lochs*, p. 222, there is an account of a blue stone near Skye on which water is poured to produce rain.

[2] *Roman de Rou*, vv. 6400 ff., ed. Andresen, pp. 284 ff. Wace's story is very simple: Hunters used to go to Bérenton and draw water. They poured a little water [by chance] on the stone, and rain followed, "I do not know why."

[8] In 1843, Benecke, in his edition of Harmann's *Iwein* (note to v. 263), compared Wace's account of Bérenton with the description of the Fountain Perilous. Maury, *Les Forêts de la Gaule*, 1867, p. 332, said that Chrétien was guided by Wace. More recently, Baist has pointed out the similarity of phrases in the two accounts (see p. 23, above).

have turned to Wace to see what he said. The question must there-fore remain undecided, with the probabilities in favor of the view that the Other-World fountain had already become rain-making and had been identified with Bérenton before Chrétien took up the story.[1]

The incident of the magic ring that renders the hero invisible is probably only a modification of some episode of the original tale, for no property of the fairies is better known than their ability to be invisible at will. On the other hand, the bleeding of the corpse in the presence of the slayer looks like a plain addition by Chrétien. The belief referred to seems to have been Germanic rather than Celtic,[2] and the probability is that the educated French poet intro-duced the incident into his narrative as a chance embellishment.

The ring which was given by Laudine to Iwain, which will release him from prison, keep him from loss of blood, and free him from all

---

[1] The origin of the rain-making power ascribed to the Fountain of Bérenton is of course a different matter. Numerous instances of fountains of the sort occur both in and out of Celtic territory. Gervase of Tilbury in his *Otia Imperialia*, written about 1212, describes (Leibnitz, I, 990; Liebrecht, pp. 41–42) a certain very clear fountain in a province of the kingdom of Arles, into which if one threw a stone, forthwith there arose a mist from the water and drenched the offender. In the same work (I, 982; Liebrecht, p. 32) there is an account of a lake on a mountain called *Cannagum* in Catalonia. No one could find the bottom of this lake, and it was regarded as the habitation of demons. "In lacum siquis aliquam lapideam aut alias solidam projecerit materiam, statim tanquam offensis daemoni-bus, tempestas erumpit." Gervase adds a story about a girl who was carried off by the demons and imprisoned for seven years in the lake. (This passage was compared with the fountain in the *Ivain* by Grimm, *Deutsche Mythologie*, 1835, p. 338; 4th ed., p. 496 and note 4.) Rain-making fountains are described by Alex-ander Neckam (1150–1227) in his *De Naturis Rerum*, bk. ii, chap. 7. Gregory of Tours (*De Gloria Confessorum*, cap. 2) has an account of libations offered at a certain lake in order to bring rain. Cf. the account in Pausanias, how a priest used to dip an oak branch in a certain water in order to procure rain (Frazer's *Pausanias*, VIII, 38). For other references, see San Marte (Alwin Schulz), *Die Arthur-Sage*, p. 153; Bellamy, *La Forêt Bréchéliant*, II, 1–32.

[2] See Grimm, *Deutsche Rechtsalterthümer*, 3d ed., pp. 930 ff.; Holland, *Crestien de Troies*, p. 157; the same, *Chev. au Lyon*, 3d ed., p. 57; P. Paris, *Romans de la Table Ronde*, I, 293, III, 378; *Hist. Litt.*, XXX, 249; Strack, *Blutaberglaube*, 1892, p. 125. Christensen's *Baareprøven*, Copenhagen, 1900, I have not yet seen. He appears to regard the idea as Celtic (cf. Herrig's *Archiv*, CVII, 109).

evil, must probably be regarded as a part of the Celtic material that came to Chrétien's hands.   It will be remembered that this ring was lost by the hero when he overstayed his time and thereby incurred the hatred of Laudine.   The messenger of Laudine appeared just at the moment when Iwain remembered that he had broken his promise :

> Et la dameisele avant saut,
> Si li oste l'anel del doi (vv. 2776–2777).

Light is thrown on this incident by a comparison of the parallel fairy mistress story of *Désiré*.   Here the *fée* gives the hero a ring by means of which he is able to control as much gold and silver as he likes.   She tells him[1]:

> Si vus meffetes de nent,
> L'anel perdrez hastivement ;
> E si ço vus seit avenu
> Ke vus aiez l'anel perdu,
> A tuz jorz mès m'avez perdue
> Sanz recoverer e sanz véue.

The hero offends the *fée* by revealing his relations with her, and, as in the case of Iwain, he forthwith loses both her and the ring.

The ring, therefore, is a gift of the *fée*, a token and an evidence of her love, and is lost the moment her displeasure is incurred.   Ahlström[2] has explained it as originally the ring that brought the *fée* to the hero whenever he desired.   A gift of this nature would naturally be taken away when the love of the *fée* was lost.   Whether Ahlström's explanation is well founded or not, it seems clear that the ring might easily be a development or a partial rationalization of some magic gift[3] made to the hero by the *fée*.   We may compare the magic ring

---

[1] Ed. Michel, *Lais Inédits*, p. 15.

[2] *Mélanges-Wahlund*, pp. 297–298.

[3] In the *Imram Brain*, for example, a magic branch of silver with white flowers is given by the *fée* to Bran.   When she desired it again "it sprang from his hand into hers, nor was there strength in Bran's hand to hold the branch."   In the modern tale *The Knight of the Green Vesture*, in *Waifs and Strays*, III, 223 ff., the *fée* gives the hero "a stone of virtues."   "There is not a virtue that thou needest for thy body that thou shalt not find as long as thou keep'st it."   It will also take

presented to Lancelot by the Lady of the Lake.[1]   On the other hand, a ring given by the heroine to protect the hero from disease and danger is a rather common feature in the romances.[2]   The possibility, therefore, that Chrétien himself introduced this incident cannot be altogether denied.

The departure of the hero after he has obtained his mistress was, as we have seen, an essential part of the typical fairy mistress story, but the motive that is assigned, — fear lest the hero should lose his fame in arms, — we may be sure is of Chrétien's own introduction. Foerster's declaration of this, with his comparison of Chrétien's earlier romance, the *Erec*, where this motive is especially dwelt on, is quite to the point.[8]   It is natural that Chrétien, in attempting to square the Celtic folk-tale to contemporary manners, should minimize the mysterious character of the lady's country and explain the hero's return by the necessity of his maintaining his fame as knight.   To Chrétien's own invention, then, may with confidence be attributed the speech put into the mouth of Gawain, in which Iwain is urged to return to Arthur's court and to the tournaments.

The helpful lion certainly seems to be of Chrétien's introduction. Upon his entrance into the plot the parallelism to the *Serglige* and the other stories of its type ceases.   Chrétien appears to have compiled the remainder of his romance chiefly from the usual chivalric material of the *chansons de geste*.   Some of the incidents of this latter part may, indeed, have belonged to a more primitive tale about Iwain (the episode of the Castle of Ill Adventure and probably also that of the Giant Harpin are in origin Celtic), but in general they bear no distinct marks of such origin.   Baist has pointed out that the

---

him in a moment whithersoever he wishes.   Similarly, in a story of Dyeermud (outlined above, p. 112, note 2), the hero is given a ring that, when he looks at it, "will keep him from cold, thirst, and hunger" (Curtin, *Hero-Tales*, p. 488).

[1] Chrétien's *Lancelot*, vv. 2348 ff.; *Merlin*, ed. Paris and Ulrich, II, 57; P. Paris, *Romans de la Table Ronde*, III, 126, IV, 80.

[2] In *King Horn* (ed. Lumby, vv. 561–576) Rymenhild gives her lover a ring that will protect him if he thinks of her (cf. Child, *Ballads*, I, 201, note).   In *Richard Coer de Leon* (Weber, *Romances*, II, 64) the hero has rings that protect from drowning and from fire.

[8] See his *Erec, Rom. Bibl.*, XIII, xvii–xviii.

latter part of the *Ivain* is much more in the chivalrous style than
the first. We begin at this point to be told of Iwain's hearing mass
in the morning, and several knightly combats in the twelfth-century
manner are introduced. The judicial battle against the Seneschal
to prove Lunete's innocence and the combat with Gawain are of this
character.

There is, therefore, no special reason to doubt that Chrétien introduced the thankful lion into the Iwain story, and a study of the
narrative seems to make this inference probable. The whole treatment of the lion is carried out *con amore*. The animal puts in an
appearance at every adventure, and his exploits are made so promi-
nent that he almost becomes for a time the real hero of the tale.
Iwain is always unable to win till the lion comes to his aid. The
extent to which this is carried seems to show that, like the psychological discussion of the motives of love in an earlier episode, the
lion is a pet idea of Chrétien's and therefore probably of his own
introduction.

The question why Chrétien introduced the precise motive of the
lion is naturally a difficult one — most probably because Iwain had
already acquired the title " Knight of the Lion " and Chrétien chose
this method of explaining it.

The title " Knight of the Lion " is one that might easily become
attached [1] to any Celtic hero because of the common custom of bearing a lion blazoned on the shield. In the *Book of Leinster*,[2] the
Dinnshenchas of Lumman Tigi Srafain (Straffan, Co. Kildare) gives
as the etymology of *lumman* (" shield ") the word *leoman* (" lion "),
because, adds the *Dinnshenchas*, " every shield has a lion on it."
The curious incident of Iwain's carrying the wounded lion in the
hollow of his shield [3] may possibly be a misunderstanding or modification of an earlier form of the tale in which the knight's shield bore

---

[1] Compare, for the custom of giving a knight a title from some animal, the
Knight of the Swan, the Knight of the Eagle (*Hist. Litt.*, XXX, 269), the Knight
of the Dragon (*Prose Perceval*, II, 19). Sir Degrevant (*Thornton Romances*,
v. 1035) had a lion on his shield.

[2] R. I. A. facsimile, p. 49.

[3] *Ivain*, vv. 4655 ff.

the figure of a lion. Moreover, a very similar explanation of Iwain's title is actually given in the *Prose Lancelot*. The story runs thus [1]:

On Easter Eve Lyonel came to King Arthur at Camelot to be knighted. A beautiful damsel presently arrived, leading a fierce lion crowned. The lion feared the damsel so much that it dared not stir. The damsel said that her lady was the loveliest in the world, but that she would marry no man except him who could slay the lion in a fight. She would not tell who her lady was. He must know it who should slay the lion. Lyonel undertook the combat. He seized the lion by the throat in his strong fists and strangled him, "*and Yvain the son of Urien carried the skin of that lion on his shield, and therefore was called li chevaliers au lyon.*" Lyonel returned with the damsel and married the lady.

If Iwain was already known as the "Knight of the Lion,"[2] it would have been natural for Chrétien to introduce the motive of the

---

[1] Summarized from an extract printed by Jonckbloet (*Le Roman de la Charrette*, pp. ix–xii, foot-note) from MS. A of the *Prose Lancelot*. MS. B reads a little differently: "Et celui jor otroia-il [Lyoniaus] la peau del' lion [à Yvein] à porter en son escu porce que messires Yveins li avoit aidié son escu à porter la veille de la Pentecoste et li avoit fet fère d'or frès."

[2] Both Rhŷs (*Arthurian Legend*, pp. 142 ff.) and Ahlström (*Mélanges-Wahlund*, pp. 299 ff.) have proposed theories to account for the connection of the title "Knight of the Lion" with Iwain, but both have deservedly met with little favor. Rhŷs's theory is, in brief, that the Welsh word *lleu* ("light") became perhaps confused with another word *llew* ("lion"), and that in this way the lion came to be regarded as a solar symbol. Since Rhŷs interprets Iwain as a sun hero, he of course thinks that solar symbols might naturally be connected with him. Ahlström's theory is almost as unconvincing. He points out that in the fairy mistress story *Guigemar*, the hero is from Léonnois, and his father is called "Sire de Liun." He thinks it possible that "Sire *de* Liun" might get changed into "Sire" or "Chevalier *au* Lion." The hero of a fairy mistress tale like Iwain might therefore be called "Chevalier au Lion." In a popular attempt to justify this title Ahlström sees the origin of the Helpful Lion story. Paris (*Romania*, XXVI, 106) rejects Ahlström's theory as being somewhat forced. It is, however, just possible that the ascription of a helpful lion to Iwain was due in part to the fact that, according to Celtic tradition, he was aided by helpful animals. Owen's ravens that fought his battles will be remembered. (See Loth, *Les Mabinogion*, II, 308, note; Lady Guest, *Mabinogion*, II, 438.) Helpful animals are a very common feature of later Celtic stories of the Journey to the Other World, and often their services come in at precisely the point where the lion enters the *Ivain*, —

thankful lion, especially as it seems to have been one which was
much to his taste. Such a motive was doubtless familiar to him
from mediæval romantic material.

Foerster has suggested[1] that the source of the incident is the lion
of Androclus. More recently, Gaidoz[2] has discussed the question at
length.

Gaidoz points out that the Bestiaries do not contain the lion
episode. He infers that the theme was brought from the Orient,
"where alone it could naturally have originated," by some crusader.
Now there was an historical crusader, Golfier de las Tours, of whom the
story is told that he saved a lion from a serpent and was afterwards
followed and aided by the lion. Gaidoz makes it appear probable
that this story existed early[3] and might have reached Chrétien's ears.[4]

---

namely, where the hero finds that he has lost his mistress and that a long series
of adventures must be gone through with in the hope of regaining her. See
Curtin, *Hero-Tales of Ireland*, p. 304, where a helpful dog appears; cf. Campbell,
Popular Tales, ed. 1860, III, 1–18, I, 165 ff. The coöperation of an animal with
his master outside of fair play is an incident found in the *Book of Leinster*. See
the account of the combat of Conall and Lugaid, *Revue Celtique*, III, 185, where
Conall's steed "Dewy Red" bites Lugaid. Cf. Cuchulinn's steed "Grey of
Macha," l.c., pp. 176–183; Henderson, *Fled Bricrend*, p. 89.

[1] *Löwenritter*, 1887, p. xxiv.

[2] *Mélusine*, V, 217–224, 241–244, VI, 74–75.

[3] The Golfier story occurs in a chronicle of 1188; see Paul Meyer, *Chanson de la
Croisade contre les Albigeois*, II, 378–380. Despite the fact that Philipot (*Annales
de Bretagne*, VIII, 56) is inclined to question Gaidoz's argument, it seems clear,
therefore, that this tradition about Golfier may have existed early enough to have
been accessible to Chrétien, though of course it cannot be regarded as certain that
it was his precise source. For the story of the faithful lion attached to certain
early saints, see Maury, *Croyances et Légendes du Moyen Age*, Paris, 1896, p. 247.
For references to the story of a lion saved from a serpent and showing his grati-
tude by following his rescuer, see Holland, *Crestien von Troies*, pp. 161–164, and
cf. *Guy of Warwick*, ed. Zupitza, E. E. T. S. (Auchinleck MS.), pp. 256–259; *Roman
de Ham*, ed. Michel, *Histoire des Ducs de Normandie*, Société de l'Histoire de
France, 1840, Index at the word *lyon*, p. 411.

[4] The carved church door from Iceland (not earlier than 1180–1190), preserved
in the Royal Museum at Copenhagen and described by Kornerup (*Mém. de la
Soc. des Antiquaires du Nord*, 1869, pp. 245 ff.), is thought by Gaidoz to portray
the story of Iwain and the lion; but Bugge (*Home of the Eddic Poems*, p. 70) is
probably right in referring it to Wolfdietrich.

The remaining incidents of the romance are most of them evidently of Chrétien's own introduction and are probably not all from the same source. The combat with giant Harpin[1] and the whole episode at the Castle of Ill Adventure seem to be of Celtic origin, and may have been attached to the story of Iwain before the time of Chrétien. There is no way of deciding the question, and it is of slight importance. A probable explanation of Chrétien's extensive insertions and additions toward the end of the romance is that he desired to bring his piece up to the length of his *Erec, Cligès,* and *Lancelot.* He may also have been unwilling to close the romance without including a little of the knightly service to ladies which was a convention of his time. Hence, perhaps, Iwain's rescue of Lunete and his combat for the Daughter of the Black Thorn.

CHAPTER VIII.

THE OTHER-WORLD LANDSCAPE IN THE ROMANCES AND LAYS.

It is convenient to bring together in this chapter various parallels found outside of Celtic literature, even though they may agree with the *Ivain* in many other points beside the landscape. In general, this motive of a marvellous landscape is likely to be the most distinct and the surest method of recognizing a rationalized Other-World story.

The most important of these parallels to the *Ivain* is probably the episode of "The Joy of the Court," in Chrétien's *Erec,*[2] a brief summary of which follows :

Erec, accompanied by his wife Enide and his friend Guivret le Petit, rides up to a château surrounded on all sides by water. It is the castle of

---

[1] Compare Arthur's fight with the Giant of Mont St. Michel (Geoffrey, x, 3).
[2] *Erec,* vv. 5367–6410.

Brandigan. Guivret advises him not to go in, because for seven years the
city has had an evil custom: those who enter must essay the adventure
of the Joy of the Court, from which no one has ever returned. Erec enters.
The people bewail him. He is magnificently entertained by the king,
Evrain, in the royal palace. On the morrow he essays the adventure.
The people again lament. There is a magic orchard enclosed " par nigro-
mance " with walls of air, so that no one can enter unless his presence is
desired. It produces flowers and fruit summer and winter; he who attempts
to carry away any of the fruit is unable to find his way out. Erec and the
multitude enter [1] this orchard by a narrow passage. They are delighted by
the song of the birds, but are horrified at the sight of pikes, on each of
which is a human head. A single pike is empty, and on this there hangs a
horn. Evrain explains that the empty pike awaits the next adventurer of
the Joy. Erec takes leave of his companions and goes forward. Beneath
a sycamore tree he finds a lovely girl on a silver bed, but he is speedily
attacked by a gigantic warrior in red armor. After a desperate conflict,
Erec is victorious. The vanquished warrior explains that his name is
Mabonagrain. He loved the lady so much that he promised her anything
she desired. She thereupon compelled him to take oath to remain with
her till some knight should vanquish him in arms. Thus she has kept him
in her magic prison for seven years. It is not his fault that the heads are
on the pikes. He has been cruel for love. Erec is told to sound the horn,
for that will be the signal of the knight's deliverance, and then the Joy will
begin. The adventure terminates by a recognition between Enide and the
beautiful lady, who is her cousin and whom she loves very much. To our
astonishment, we have no definite explanation as to what the Joy of the
Court really is.

No one can read this summary, — still less, the original text of the
episode, — without feeling confident that it is not, in its present form,
the creation of any one man's fancy. Its confusions and irrationalities could only have resulted from the distortion of an earlier
supernatural tale.[2] Every one wishes to know how the name " La

---

[1] The entrance of the whole multitude spoils the mystery of the wall of air.
An earlier form of the episode must have been different.

[2] The confusion of this episode has been so clearly brought out by Paris
(*Romania*, XX, 148–166) and by Philipot (*Romania*, XXV, 258–294) that I
need only refer to some of the more glaring irrationalities. Paris and Philipot
agree that it is a distorted fairy mistress story of the type of the *Ivain*.

Joie de la Cort" originated [1]; what the magic wall of air and the horn are for; why the persons concerned, and especially Evrain, are so much pleased at having the enchantment ended; and, above all, how Enide can love the beautiful lady so dearly, when it is clear that it is the jealous passion and the ferocity of this same lady that have brought about the whole adventure, including the utter savagery of the heads on pikes. These enigmas are insoluble if the episode be considered by itself; but they may all be explained if it be regarded as a partly rationalized fairy mistress story, parallel to the *Ivain*.[2]

The scene of the adventure is on an island. This brings it close to the *Condla*, the *Bran*, and the *Serglige*, and suggests a comparison with the Welsh Isle of Avalon. The royal entertainer, Evrain, who feasts the hero splendidly, is a parallel figure to the Hospitable Host in the *Ivain*. Both entertain the hero for the night, and in the morning send him forth to the adventure of the Other World.[3] The scene of Erec's adventure is enclosed by a magic wall of air, so that no one can enter, any more than if it were surrounded with iron. There is, however, " une estroite antrée," evidently a trace of the Perilous Passage motive, by which the place may be reached. The interior is an orchard, and the trees have the well-known unfading quality of the Other World :

> Et tot esté et tot iver
> I avoit flors et fruit meür (vv. 5746–5747).[4]

---

[1] Paris supposes that this name is due to some mistranslation. Philipot connects it with the Irish *Inis-Subai* (île de Joie), a name applied in *Condla*, § 6, and *Bran*, § 63, to ine Other World.

[2] The apparent ferocity of the lady is merely a survival of her primitive supernatural character. No adventurer surmounts the perils of the passage to the Other World except the one chosen by the *fée*.

[3] Probably the Hospitable Host in the *Ivain* originally directed the hero to the scene of the adventure, much as Evrain does.

[4] Cf. *Ivain*, vv. 384–385 :

> An toz tans la fuelle li dure,
> Qu'il ne le pert por nul iver.

The orchard abounds in the singing birds of the Other World :

> Ne soz ciel n'a oisel volant
> Qui pleise a home, qui n'i chant
> Por lui deduire et resjoïr,
> Que l'an n'an i peüst oïr
> Plusors de chascune nature (vv. 5755 ff.).

Erec experiences the same joy at the singing of the birds that Iwain feels at the Fountain Perilous :

> Qui mout se delitoit el chant
> Des oisiaus qui leanz chantoient (vv. 5770–5771).

Erec advances alone, just as Calogrenant does [1] in the *Ivain* :

> Seus, sanz conpeignie de jant (v. 5879),

and finds a beautiful girl

> Dessoz l'onbre d'un sicamor (v. 5882).

Near by, on an empty pike, hangs a horn.

It will be observed that we have here almost all the important features of the Other-World landscape. Though much confused, the scene is evidently in one respect more primitive than that in the *Ivain*, — it lacks the rather absurd method of challenge by pouring water on a rock and thus provoking a terrible storm.[2]

Light is thrown on this episode by comparing the incident of the Castle of Ill Adventure in the *Ivain*.[8] Both are extremely confused rationalizations of visits to the Other World. As Iwain approaches the Castle of Ill Adventure, the people by the roadside bewail his fate. After he has passed an abusive porter, he comes to a row of pikes :

> S'avoit devant un prael clos
> De peus aguz, reonz et gros (vv. 5191–5192).

---

[1] Cf. *Ivain*, vv. 176–177 :

> Que je seus come païsanz
> Aloie querant avantures.

[2] The close parallel between the giant knight Mabonagrain, clad in red armor, and Esclados the Red should be noticed (cf. p. 116).

[8] See vv. 5107–5770.

It is not said that there are any heads on the pikes, but the analogy of the Joy of the Court episode and of a multitude of Other-World [1] stories makes this a fair inference. This idea is confirmed by the fact that every man entertained at the castle is obliged in the morning to fight for his life against two goblins, — a state of affairs that must have furnished a good supply of heads. It is in an orchard, as in the *Erec*, that the hero finally finds the inhabitants, — a beautiful maiden and her father and mother. As Evrain plays the part of the Hospitable Host in the *Erec*, so these three entertain Iwain sumptuously :

> De lui servir tant s'antremet
> Qu'il an a honte et si l'an poise (vv. 5430–5431).

Nevertheless, in the morning the maiden's father involves Iwain in a mortal combat with the goblins, somewhat as Evrain led Erec to the duel in the orchard.

It is distinctly stated in the *Ivain* that the combat is required. Every knight who is entertained must fight. There are many hints that this must have been originally the case in the Joy of the Court. It is a part of the custom of the Castle of Ill Adventure that, if the knight slays the goblins, he is to have the lovely daughter to wife. Iwain has some difficulty in escaping from this requirement. Similarly, we may be sure that in the Joy of the Court (as in the combat at the Fountain Perilous), the conquering hero originally won the hand of the *fée*.[2]

---

[1] The heads on pikes have been observed in the *Tale of Curoi* and in *La Mule sans Frein*. Examples of this motive have been collected in Child's *Ballads*, V, 482, and by Schofield, *Harvard Studies and Notes*, IV, 175 ff. To the many references cited in these places I may add one Celtic example of great antiquity, in the *Siaburcharpat Conculaind* from the *Lebor na h-Uidre*. When Cuchulinn visited the Land of Scath (shadow), he saw a rampart of irons, on which were seven heads. See O'Beirne Crowe, *Proceedings of Royal Hist. and Arch. Assoc. of Ireland*, 4th series, I, 387 (1871). Modern Celtic examples, not before collected, are: Curtin, *Hero-Tales*, pp. 66, 214, 381 ; Hyde, *Beside the Fire*, p. 39 ; Yeats, *Irish Fairy Tales*, p. 177 ; Larminie, *West Irish Folk-Tales*, pp. 158, 207 ; *Celtic Magazine*, XIII, 25 ; *Zt. f. celt. Phil.*, I, 488 ; cf. Groome, *Gypsy Folk-Tales*, p. 257.

[2] The connection indicated (vv. 5257 ff.) between the Castle of Ill Adventure and "l'Isle as Puceles" is worth noting. The Isle of Maidens is an ancient Celtic name for the Other World.

Both in the episode of the Castle of Ill Adventure and in that of the
Joy of the Court emphasis is laid on the universal rejoicing when the
hero breaks up the marvellous custom.

By comparing these two episodes, then, we see that, in an earlier
and more complete form of the type of story which they represent,
the hero must have been entertained by a hospitable host, who in
the morning led him to the adventure of the Other World.   The
heads of previous adventurers were on pikes about the place.   The
hero overthrew a supernatural opponent (a goblin or *netun*) and won
the hand of a *fée*.   In their original form, the stories were evidently
close parallels to the *Serglige* and the *Ivain*.

It is interesting to note that the poetic insight of Hartmann von
Aue seems to have enabled him to recognize the true Other-World
character both of the scene in the Joy of the Court and of the
corresponding scene at the Fountain Perilous.   In both cases he
compares the place to Paradise.   In his *Erec* he makes the beautiful
damsel say to her lover :

> Ouoh wil ich mich vermezzen,
> Wir haben hie besezzen
> *Daz ander paradîse.*[1]
> Die selben stat ich prîse
> Für alle boumgarten.
> Als ir selbe muget warten,
> Hie ist inne michel wünne
> Von aller vogel künne
> Und von missevarwer bluot:
> Hie wær' daz wesen inne guot (vv. 9539 ff.).

In his description of the Fountain Perilous in his *Iwein* he inserts
the lines :

> Alsus het ich besezzen
> *Daz ander pardîse* (vv. 686–687).

---

[1] Kölbing (*Zt. f. vergleich. Litteraturgeschichte*, XI, 442–448) has with great
probability explained this phrase as meaning the Earthly Paradise, as distinguished
from the *first* (or heavenly) paradise.   He has also compared the Swedish *Herr
Ivan* (vv. 438–439) : " Mik thokte . . . iak vare ij Paradiis."

That this addition of Hartmann's is not due to mere chance appears probable from a comparison of *Le Tournoiement d'Anté-christ*,[1] a poem written about the year 1235 by Huon de Méry. Huon avowedly used Chrétien's *Ivain* as a sort of model. In his poem he tells us that he went to the Fountain in the wood of Berceliande and found everything just as Chrétien described it. He poured water on the stone. The storm followed. After this the birds sang so sweetly that it seemed to him "que c'est terrïens paradis" (v. 202). He adds:

> Li services [of the birds] fu beax et lons,
> Qu'il firent a lour crïatour (vv. 208–209).

After this a "Mor" appeared. The cowardly Huon surrendered to this antagonist, whom he was obliged to follow to the city of Despair (Deseperance). "Li Mors" is called "Bras de fer" and is "d'Enfer"; he is, indeed, one of the lieutenants of Satan. The poem from this point becomes a sort of vision. Huon is taken to behold a great tournament between the forces of Satan and the hosts of the Lord.

It is unlikely that Huon de Méry, writing about seventy years later, understood better than Chrétien the landscape at the Fountain Perilous.[2] He seems, however, to have connected it, not, of course, directly with Celtic stories, but with monkish vision-literature, in which, as has been shown in the case of the *Visio Tnugdali* and the *Owain Miles*, the conventional landscape of the Celtic Other World distinctly appears. Many cases of its occurrence in visions of the Earthly Paradise could be collected.[8]

---

[1] Ed. Wimmer, in Stengel's *Ausgaben und Abhandlungen*, 1888, LXXVI; cf. ed. Tarbé, Reims, 1851.

[2] Huon's lines establish with absolute certainty Kölbing's translation of "feire servise" (*Ivain*, vv. 471–472), which has been adopted above (p. 87). I base no argument on the fact that Huon evidently regards the Fountain Perilous as an entrance to the Lower World, though this is possibly a significant matter. A writer of distinctly monastic tendencies like Huon would naturally identify the fairies with spirits of evil.

[8] See, for example, the *Metrical Life of St. Brandan*, ed. Wright, pp. 9 ff.; *Tundale*, ed. Wagner, pp. 114–115. Episodes and tales that contain traces of the Other-World landscape and are perhaps in origin rationalized fairy stories are

Distinct traces of the Other-World landscape appear in the lays of
Guingamor, Graelent, Lanval, and *Désiré.* These are all fairy
mistress stories, and resemble each other so much that a single brief
summary will illustrate the group : The hero, wandering solitary in
the wilderness, comes to a fountain or a river, where he meets a *fée.*
He wins her love and remains with her for a time. At length he
leaves her land and returns to dwell again amongst men. The *fée,*
however, has put some command upon him, which he breaks and
thereby loses her and her love. He falls into the most profound
grief, so that after a period of suffering the *fée* at last takes pity on
him and brings him back to live in her land forever.[1]

The scene where Guingamor finds the *fée* is as follows[2] :

> Enz el chief de la lande entra ;
> Une fontaine illec trova
> Desoz un olivier foillu
> Vert et flori et bien branchu :
> La fontaingne ert et clére et bele,
> D'or et d'argent ert la gravele ;
> Une pucele s'i baingnoit,
>
> .   .   .   .
>
> Sor un grant arbre vit ses dras (vv. 421 ff.).

In *Graelent*[3] the description is briefer :

> Tant qu'en une lande l'an maine,
> Devers le sors d'une fontaine
> Dunt l'iare esteit è clere è bele
> Dedens baigneit une pucele (p. 502).

---

common in mediæval literature. See [*Chaucer's*] *Dream* (Bell's *Chaucer*, London,
1878, III, vv. 439–508); *Romania*, X, 474 (where an episode from the *Lanzelet* of
Ulrich von Zatzikhoven is quoted); *Hist. Litt.*, XXX, 86 ff. (where the romance
of *Rigomer* is analyzed). Professor Kittredge has called my attention to an
episode in *Wolfdietrich B*, sts. 350 ff., which contains not only the landscape, but
the combat motive in a form that suggests the *Ivain.*

[1] It will be observed that this summary would apply fairly well to the *Ivain.*
The absence of the fighting motive, however, marks the lays as belonging to a
different type of fairy story.

[2] Ed. Paris, *Romania*, VIII, 50–59.

[3] Ed. Roquefort, *Poésies de Marie*, I, 486–541. (The lay is not really by

In *Lanval*[1] we read :

> Tuz suls est en un pre venuz.
> Sur une ewe curant descent;
> Mes sis chevals tremble forment:
> Il le descengle, si s'en vait
>
> . . . .
>
> La u il gist en tel maniere,
> Guarda a val lez la riviere,
> Si vit venir dous dameiseles (vv. 44 ff.).

In *Désiré*[2] it is said :

> A une funteine veneit
> Ke suz un grant arbre surdeit;
> Dous bacins d'or tent en ses meins.

This lay of *Désiré* is the closest parallel to the *Ivain*, because in it there is an attendant damsel who plays a part similar to that of Lunete, acting as intermediary between the hero and the *fée*. In this lay also there is a parallel to the ring given by Laudine to Iwain.

The continuation of Chrétien's *Perceval* by Gaucher embodies a number of incidents that are perhaps in origin Other-World tales parallel to the *Ivain*. In vv. 23,292 ff.[3] we are told how Perceval entered an empty castle, by which in a beautiful meadow was a fountain and a cypress tree. After slaying a lion he finds a maiden. He is obliged to overcome a knight called Abrioris. In vv. 23,880 ff. Perceval crosses a bridge and finds a beautiful tree and an empty

---

Marie.) Cf. *Ivain*, vv. 422 ff. :

> De la fontaine poez croire
> Qu'ele boloit com iaue chaude.
> Li perrons iert d'une esmeraude,
> Perciez aussi com une boz,
> Si ot quatre rubiz desoz
> Plus flanboianz et plus vermauz
> Que n'est au matin li solauz.

[1] Ed. Warnke, *Lais der Marie*, 2d ed., p. 88.

[2] Ed. Michel, *Lais Inédits*, p. 11. On these lays, see Schofield, *Harvard Studies and Notes*, V, 221 ff., and *Publications of the Mod. Lang. Assoc. of America*, XV, 121 ff.

[3] Ed. Potvin; cf. vv. 15,426 ff., 22,397 ff.

tower. A girl who is thin and pale at length appears. A giant has kept her captive for over two years and wishes to marry her. Perceval, whose horse the giant kills, fights him and at last slays him. In vv. 26,496 ff. Perceval crosses a water and comes to a castle apparently empty. He strikes on a "table . . . d'arain ovrée" with a hammer that hangs by a silver chain, and finally maidens appear and entertain him. It is the Castle of Maidens. He is led to the chamber of the lady of the castle. In the morning he finds that the castle has vanished. He meets a knight, Garsalas, whose brother once found by a fountain a *fée*, who took him to this mysterious castle, where he spent ten years with her. He was called "Li Noirs Chevaliers de Valdoune."

There is in the Prose *Tristan*[1] what appears to be a confused fairy mistress tale parallel to the *Ivain*, in which a character called Mennonas[2] appears playing very much the part taken in the ancient Celtic stories by Manannán. A beautiful woman is discovered in an island at a fountain, and Mennonas and Mabon contend for her possession. Mabon, eager to be rid of Mennonas, sends a *nef de joie* to Cornwall to secure the help of Tristan. Tristan enters the marvellous vessel and is conducted to the " Isle of the Fountain," where he goes through an adventure almost exactly like that of Iwain at the Fountain Perilous. His adversary is called Ferrant (Pharant).

This incident in the *Tristan* has probably been influenced by Chrétien's *Ivain;* but, if it is based entirely on Chrétien's romance, the changes made are certainly of a very extraordinary character. It seems more probable that it is in origin an ancient tale.

Finally, there is in Malory's *Morte Darthur* a partly rationalized fairy mistress story curiously parallel to the *Ivain*[3]:

A damsel comes into Arthur's hall and prays for succor. " I have a lady of grete worship and renomme, and she is byseged with a tyraunte so that she may not oute of her castel." " What heteth your lady and where

---

[1] Löseth, *Tristan*, pp. 247 ff. This passage was pointed out to me by Dr. Schofield.

[2] Spelled also *Manonas*.

[3] The story runs through Malory's seventh book, the source of which has not yet been pointed out. I refer to Sommer's edition, pp. 215–272.

dwelleth she, and who is he and what is his name that hath byseged her ? " "Syre kyng," she saide, "as for my ladyes name that shall not ye knowe for me as at this tyme. . . . As for the tyraunt that bysyegeth her . . . he is called the rede knyght of the reed laundes. . . . He hath seven mennys strengthe." "Fayre damoysel," sayd the kynge, "there ben knyʒtes here wolde doo her power for to rescowe your lady, but by cause ye wylle not telle her name, nor where she dwelleth, therfor none of my knyghtes that here be now shal goo with you by my wylle " (p. 216).

Gareth, who is called Beaumains, and has just come to court, undertakes the adventure. The damsel's name is Lynet. She is sister to her lady, who is Dame Lyonesse (p. 235), and lives in the " Yle of Avylyon (p. 255). The Red Knight, whose name is Ironsyde, is challenged by blowing a horn that hangs by a sycamore near the sea (p. 236). The bodies of many knights, who have failed in the adventure, are to be seen hanging on trees. Gareth conquers the Red Knight, but the fair Lyonesse refuses to receive him till he has been enrolled among the number of worthy knights. Gareth is so distressed by this thatthe rides " thorou marys and feldes and grete dales . . . for he knewe not the wey, but took the gaynest waye in that woodenes that many tymes he was lyke to perysshe " (p. 243). The Damsel Lyonesse, however, takes pity on him, and he is lured back to her castle by her brother Gryngamore. But when Gareth becomes too forward in his love, Lynet conjures up an armed knight to attack him. Gareth slays the knight and hacks him into small pieces, but the damsel Lynet puts him together again as well as ever, and also heals Gareth's wounds (p. 249).

Gareth now decides to depart, in order to engage in a tournament. Dame Lyonesse presents him with a ring that will keep him from losing blood and give him the power of changing color, so that he may not be known (p. 257). Gareth has a number of adventures, in one of which, by over-coming a hostile knight, he frees thirty ladies who are imprisoned in a castle (p. 266). His final adventure is a single combat with Gawain (pp. 267 ff.), in which the heroes at last recognize each other. Immediately after this combat we are told how Gareth finds again the Lady Lyonesse and marries her at the Castle Perilous beside the Isle of "Avylyon."

It is fair to say that, as this story is given in Malory, it is confused by a number of intervening adventures omitted in the above sum-mary. The parallel to the *Ivain* is, however, unmistakable. The name and character of Lynet, and that of the Red Knight, who must be overcome before the mysterious lady can be reached, are enough by themselves to establish the parallel.

There are a number of points in which this late tale preserves more primitive incidents than those in the *Ivain*, as our study of the Ancient Celtic Other-World stories makes clear. The coming of a messenger from a mysterious land whose name she is unwilling to disclose closely parallels the coming of Liban in the *Serglige*. As Arthur's knights show reluctance to accompany Lynet, so Cuchulinn did not desire to go on a woman's invitation. An incident of this kind is only hinted at in the *Ivain*. Lynet in Malory is the sister of the lady, just as Liban was to Fand. The *Ivain* does not mention such a relation between Lunete and Laudine. The mode of challenging the Red Knight by blowing a horn appears to be simpler and more primitive than the Rain-Making Fountain features of the *Ivain*. The power of conjuring up supernatural warriors who must be overcome but are not really killed, ascribed to Lynet (and therefore by inference to her lady), is exactly the power that the primitive *fée* must have had. The ring presented by Dame Lyonesse to Gareth, which gives him the power of changing color so that he cannot be recognized, reminds us of the shape-shifters in Other-World story, from Manannán to Avartach of the Many-Colored Raiment. It is noticeable, too, that there is no thankful lion in Malory's episode.

Is this, then, a confused survival of a form of the tale of Iwain older than that told by Chrétien? When one considers the close parallelism that must have existed between many Celtic Other-World tales of the same type, such an hypothesis seems unlikely. At several points, for example, the tale in Malory agrees with the Joy of the Court Episode, as opposed to the *Ivain:* e.g., in mentioning the relics of former adventurers placed about the scene of combat, and in describing the tree at the place of challenge as a sycamore.[1] It is more likely, therefore, that we have in Malory a late and extremely confused form of an ancient Celtic Other-World tale which some transcriber, noticing its resemblances to the *Ivain*, has worked over to make the resemblance still closer, and that this redactor has named the lady's messenger Lynet.

---

[1] See *Erec*, v. 5882 :

Dessoz l'onbre d'un sicamor.

In view of the repeated appearance in the later romances[1] of these apparent survivals of Celtic tradition, not all of which can reasonably be ascribed to chance, it seems fair to infer that there were once in existence, and known to the French romancers, numbers of Celtic Other-World tales, parallel to the *Ivain*, which have now been lost.

CHAPTER IX.

CONCLUSION.

THIS investigation has shown that parallels to every important incident of the main portion of Chrétien's *Ivain*, namely, the portion extending from the beginning to the appearance of the lion, — are found[2] in ancient Celtic stories belonging to one clearly defined type. Most of the themes thus traced appear united in a single Irish Other-World tale, the *Serglige Conculaind*.[3] In the case of the more important of these themes, such as The Giant Herdsman, The Other-World Landscape, Marriage with the Widow of the Slain Warrior, and The Broken Promise and Madness, the parallels are of the most significant character. No reasonable doubt can remain that the main portion of the *Ivain* is at bottom a Celtic Other-World tale of the type represented by the *Serglige*. Numerous parallel fairy mistress

---

[1] E.g., "Li Noirs Chevaliers de Valdoune" (Avalon), p. 142, above; the mysterious character, "Mennonas" or "Manonas" (Manannán?), p. 142; and the numerous cases just pointed out in Malory's story.

[2] Except the rain-making character of the fountain. It has been shown, however, that the Other-World Fountain was apt to pass into a mere magic fountain (see *Mailduin*, § 20); and the localization of the story at Bérenton, which probably happened before Chrétien, will account for the precise rain-making features. On marvellous fountains, cf. Louis de Nussac, *Les Fontaines en Limousin, Culte, Pratiques, Légendes*, in *Bulletin Archéologique du Comité des Travaux historiques et scientifiques*, 1897, pp. 150–177.

[3] The proof, it will be observed, rests on the ancient tales. The chapter on modern Celtic parallels is meant to be corroborative only.

stories, partly rationalized (such as the Joy of the Court episode in the *Erec*), furnish all the auxiliary evidence that can be fairly expected.

This view is supported, not only by a host of parallels, but by the fact that it alone will explain all the inconsequences and inconsistencies of the present form of the *Ivain*, which, if the tale be regarded as Chrétien's invention, one is obliged most unjustifiably to neglect. Any other theory is compelled to regard the entire romance as essentially a jumble of incidents, arranged without any definite thread of connection.

That such an hypothesis about the *Ivain* should ever have been entertained is due to the fact that the original character of the story has been considerably confused, and that towards the end a number of adventures *do* seem to have been introduced, the present arrangement of which is almost entirely accidental.

These disconnected adventures are to be explained in the following way. The analogy of stories like the ancient tale of *Loegaire* and of well-nigh all the later Celtic tales, supported by the general presumption that almost any story will in time acquire a happy ending, leads one to suppose that the ultimate reconciliation of Iwain to Laudine, and probably also a journey of wonderful adventure that led him back to her land, formed a part of the Celtic material that Chrétien used. Chrétien has evidently kept but few of the original adventures that led up to the reconciliation, but has substituted for them others better suited to the taste of his time. In particular, he has introduced the brilliant decorative feature of the Thankful Lion. This motive he has interwoven with some skill into all the adventures that follow, except the combat with Gawain, of which it would manifestly have spoiled the point.

The *Ivain* has then but one source, a Celtic Other-World tale, which had been slightly modified by the addition of rain-making features to the fountain. Chrétien has rationalized this tale so far as it was possible and has dressed it up in the costume of the twelfth century. He has made the warriors knights in armor, and the *fée* a courtly lady. In the latter part of the tale he has inserted several conventional knightly combats to please the taste of the age of chivalry and has interwoven the favorite theme of the thankful lion.

This view does not represent Chrétien as having made up the *Ivain* out of his own fancy, nor as having compiled it from various entirely disconnected sources; but it does credit him with having put upon almost every line of the poem the imprint of his own personality. The intricate discussion of motive by which Laudine's change of mind is sought to be explained, shows the touch of the twelfth century *trouvère*. The touching, if to our notions somewhat naïve, pathos of the grateful lion reveals the handiwork of the well-informed courtly poet.

This view leaves a scope for Chrétien's activity really as great as that occupied by Tennyson in the composition of the *Idylls of the King*. Chrétien made over a fairy tale into a chivalric romance ; Tennyson has made over chivalric romances into allegories with mystic meaning. Each has read into older material the ideas of his own day.

Our problem in determining the sources of Chrétien is something like that which one may imagine a scholar about the year 2500 might have in ascertaining the sources of Tennyson's *Idylls*, if we could suppose that all of the older literature about Arthur had perished with the exception of a limited number of French romances, none of which chanced to contain any of the precise stories put into English verse by Tennyson. Absolute demonstration in a problem of this sort is evidently impossible. It is believed, however, that the theory of a Celtic origin for the story of the *Ivain* has been shown to possess extraordinary probability, — a probability far greater than should be enough to determine its general acceptance.